ART OF THE REAL

ART OF THE REAL

Nine American Figurative Painters

Edited by Mark Strand

FOREWORD BY ROBERT HUGHES

PHOTOGRAPHS BY TIMOTHY GREENFIELD-SANDERS

Clarkson N. Potter, Inc./Publishers

DISTRIBUTED BY CROWN PUBLISHERS, INC.

NEW YORK

Published by Clarkson N. Potter, Inc., One Park Avenue, New York, New York 10016 and simultaneously in Canada by General Publishing Company Limited

Manufactured in Japan by Toppan Printing Co., Inc.

Library of Congress Cataloging in Publication Data

Strand, Mark, 1934–
    The art of the real.

    1. Figurative art—United States.   2. Realism in art—United States.   3. Painting, American.   4. Painting, American.   I. Greenfield-Sanders, Timothy.
II. Title.
ND212.5.F5S77   1983   759.13 [B]   83–4034
ISBN 0–517–54759–7

10 9 8 7 6 5 4 3 2 1
First Edition

Contents

Acknowledgments

I am grateful to the artists for giving their valuable time to this project; to my editors, Carol Southern (whose idea this book was) and Kathy Powell, for their continuing support and interest; and to Jeri Schneider, who handled the typing of the transcripts with patience, good humor, and intelligence. I would also like to thank Jane Schoelkopf of the Robert Schoelkopf Gallery, George Adams of the Allan Frumkin Gallery, Melinda Tally of Davis & Langdale Company, Jody Cutler of Fischbach Gallery, Joan Wolff of the Allan Stone Gallery, and Terry Hubscher of Marlborough Gallery for providing transparencies and information about the paintings.

M. S.

Foreword

American art criticism has its discreet code words. One, often heard in the last few years, is "the revival of realism." It politely suggests that realist painting fainted, or perhaps died, for a couple of decades; whereas now it issues from its tomb like Lazarus, joyfully to be greeted by (among others) critics. This construction has one great advantage. It sidles past the embarrassing question of fashion, to which no group of people, least of all the labile crowd that constitutes the art world, is immune.

The truth, of course, is that realist painting in America did not hibernate in the 50s, and was not woken in the 80s. Instead, people stopped looking at it because they felt they ought only, or mainly, to be looking at abstract art or Pop. The art world thought realism was old-fashioned, and to cover its mistake it now talks about revivals. It believed that, whatever happened among the eddies and reeds at its edges, the mainstream of modern art flowed toward reduction, to abstraction. (This led to some striking casuistries, such as the treatment of Willem de Kooning—a painter as obsessed with the human figure as any American in the last fifty years—as an *abstract* expressionist.) Images of the real world were approved to the extent that they could be treated as signs, demonstrations of linguistic interplay and irony, as in Pop; but in general, the dogma was that only abstraction contained higher seriousness and pointed to the future.

Moreover, people naively liked to disparage realism by comparing it to photography—which can only be done if one studies neither. If a photo can give you Truth at f/16 at $\frac{1}{250}$, who needs realist painting? But the operations of painter and photographer—one incessantly criticizing the motifs and translating them into visual codings by hand, the other editing and selecting what the passive lens will scoop up—are essentially different. We are all soaked in photographic imagery from birth. We take it, and its intrusions, for granted. But only since the 70s has a large audience started to look *critically* at photographs, and this may well explain why there has been a shift in interest back to realist painting. Only scrutiny reveals the fundamental differences between the two forms.

When dogmas fail, questions are asked. When the imposing orthodoxy of late modernism began to show its cracks in the late 60s, people began to wonder what happened to realism; and two things became apparent. The first was that the kind of teaching based squarely on figure-drawing, which in the nineteenth century created the cultural ground—the general graphic literacy, so to speak—for a Degas or a Matisse on that side of the Atlantic, or an Eakins or Homer on this, no longer existed. The ''academic'' base of realism had largely been destroyed. American artists had to re-invent the figure for themselves, using whatever prototypes they could. The second thing, however, was that there were in America a number of stubborn talents busy doing just that. None of them harbored Oedipal resentment against the achievements of an older generation, the father figures, the abstract ex-pressionists. The work of a Pearlstein or a Welliver is suffused with intelligent references to their predecessors' paintings. Nevertheless they were all, in their various ways, committed to doing what many people thought culturally impossible; and the extent to which they succeeded can be gauged, in part, from the reproductions in this book. To read these artists on their own art is to realize how deceptive the surface of ''realism'' can be—what complexities of decision and paradoxes of insight it must assimilate—and to be reminded that, in the end, what a painter says about his or her life and ideas is apt to cast more light on the work than ten yards of critical prose. I feel grateful to Mark Strand for talking to them and so instructing me.

Robert Hughes

Introduction

It was during the late forties and early fifties, when American painting was dominated by abstract expressionist and color-field painting, that the painters in *Art of the Real* began their careers. From the beginning they favored a direction in which the world of recognizable objects was depicted. Within an unreceptive critical climate, one that held that theirs was a minor and outmoded genre, a throwback to anti-modernist aesthetics, they remained committed to representation, which is to say they were committed to paying close attention to what was around them, whether it was the highly nuanced character of light or the more obvious order of figure and ground. It is this attention that has the power of compensating for our ever increasing sense of estrangement from the natural world. One of the shared assumptions in the work of the artists in *Art of the Real* is that our relationship to the physical world, a relationship that is perpetually in danger of being destroyed by inattention, can be salvaged. Again and again, we see in their work the world in all its variety not merely alluded to but revealed, with visual incident becoming illumination.

In the early sixties, when public attention shifted away from experiments in abstraction and focused on pop art, representation was once again an accepted mode of painting. But pop art, because it relied on an imagery created by popular culture and dominated by consumer goods, was very different in character from the figurative painting that was then going on. In its short life, pop art was an influence only on photo realism. The nine figurative painters in *Art of the Real* owe nothing to pop art. Believing in the selective and psychological attributes of the human eye as opposed to the camera eye, they do not work from photographs, nor do they care about reproducing the glossy neutrality of the photographic image. They are more concerned with the manipulation of surface as it serves the creation of a convincing illusionistic space. The exactitude to which they subscribe addresses the particular harmony they wish to establish between what they see and how they wish it to be seen, and not the exhaustive rendering of topographic details. The photo realists' reliance on the camera gives their paintings a crisp, oddly hygienic quality that makes them look alike, a quality that is carried even further by the leveling effect of the airbrush.

By contrast, the work of the more painterly figurative painters manifests a variety of attitudes toward subject matter; their individuality reflected in the ways they apply paint to canvas with a brush, energetically transforming the ordinary into the memorable. Despite these differences—and there are more in the full range of contemporary figurative painting—the assumption persists in show after show that all forms of so-called realism are compatible, that there is no need to distinguish the confusing and contradictory modes of representation brought together under that appellation. Thus, all the *realisms*—photo, neo, allegorical, painterly, and so on—are lumped together with the implicit understanding that if the shapes seen on canvas bear some relation to objects seen in the world, a realist painting is what we are looking at.

If the figurative painters in *Art of the Real* have little to do with pop art or photo realism, they also have little to do with the regional, optimistic, and politically reductive representational painting that flourished in America prior to World War II. Nor do they have anything to do with the representational painting that was done just after the war by an older generation of figurative painters—those symbolic, demoralized views of mankind imprisoned or lost in a relentlessly bleak world. In fact, with the exception of Jack Beal, the painters in this book are not concerned with the sort of social messages which, from the time of Courbet, have been associated with realism. They are committed, rather, to figuration as a mode that holds its own value; they respect the formal considerations of modernism and are drawn to the painterly conventions of abstract expressionism.

When these artists speak about their own work, it is clear that they have responded to a variety of precursors, that they have established for themselves traditions in which their work achieves not only historical coherence but a newness that is more than mere novelty. Tradition—to paraphrase T. S. Eliot—is not inherited but is something obtained by great labor. The painters in *Art of the Real* paint not only with a feeling for their own present but with a sense that the

whole history of art "has a simultaneous existence and composes a simultaneous order." Alex Katz, for instance, traces his influences from Egyptian painting, through Watteau, to Matisse. Lennart Anderson traces his from Pompeian painting, through Poussin and Ingres, to Degas and Edwin Dickinson. Their choices allow them to exist more powerfully in the present. Almost all the painters in *Art of the Real* pay homage to the great generation of abstract expressionists that immediately preceded them, a curious fact when one considers their differences. Whereas for the abstract expressionists a painting could be justified as the lavish chronicle of its becoming, a painterly projection of the shapeless, mysterious territory of the self, the figurative painters were less self-conscious, less given to the romanticizing of process. They pursue—in their concern with, and restoration of, illusionistic space—an objectivity that not only recognizes the world around them but also depends on it. Their paintings are not projections of self-discovery so much as evidence of a varied and on-going engagement with the world.

The selection of painters in *Art of the Real* was a personal one arrived at after long discussions with my editor. Finally, it seemed that the first generation of figurative painters after abstract expressionism should be set apart from others with whom they were often indiscriminately grouped. The desire for an ample selection of each painter's work (and even with these nine, one wishes for more) and the limitations imposed by the projected length of the book meant that many exceptional painters of that generation were excluded—Leland Bell, Alfred Leslie, Gabriel Laderman, Jane Wilson, Paul Georges, Nell Blaine, among others. By the same token, had it been possible to include members of the younger generation of figurative painters—Janet Fish, Rackstraw Downes, Paul Wiesenfeld, John Moore, William Beckman, Catherine Murphy, some of whom were students of those included here—I would have done so.

The text of *Art of the Real* is an edited version of

taped transcripts of interviews I conducted with the painters. The casual autobiographical format became an editorial imperative, since it seemed to elicit the greatest amount of information with the least amount of self-consciousness. And because it seemed best to have the artists speak for themselves about their work and careers, and to have them do so in a unified, uninterrupted series of disclosures, there was no need to retain the editor's questions. The editor's job was to shape and clarify the responses of the painters so that they could be read with maximum pleasure.

June 1983

Mark Strand

William Bailey

As a child, I drew all the time—I think partly because we moved around so much. I was born in Council Bluffs, Iowa, a town right across the Missouri River from Omaha, Nebraska. My father was in the radio business in the early days of broadcasting, and during the Depression we moved from one radio station to another. We lived in Chicago (two or three times), Detroit, Kansas City, Muskogee, and a half a dozen other places. I read a lot and would illustrate things that I was reading. I was also a moviegoer, and I drew things that I remembered from the movies.

During my airplane stage I did drawings for *Dawn Patrol*. Most of the kids could do only side views. But I could do three-quarter views, which set me ahead. I was very interested in American history, and my father had a set of books that were a fictionalized account of American history, with one family going through the Revolutionary War, the War of 1812, and so on. I illustrated all of those wars and also the opening of the West. If I was asked at that time what I wanted to be when I grew up I would have said an artist.

I was not praised or encouraged at school. Drawing was always a very private thing for me. When I was in high school in Kansas City, there was one art teacher who had terrible taste but was encouraging, even though I didn't do the kind of work that she liked. Her idea of art was something that might be suitable for the greeting-card business. The Hallmark Company was in Kansas City, and she was always telling me, "Well, you have a real talent but you've never used it." And so I took art in high school for only a year or two, but I worked on my own and all that time felt that I was going to be an artist. Then I went to the University of Kansas School of Fine Arts. I was supposed to be studying commercial art, which they called design. There was also a department of drawing and painting, and as soon as I found out about it, that's where I went. I took all the drawing courses that they offered and as much painting as possible.

There was an office there where all the journals and art magazines were laid out, and I would go in and look through them. My great heros at that time were El Greco, Rembrandt, Goya, Titian, Giorgione, Caravaggio, and other old masters, but then I was also terribly excited by contemporary painting.

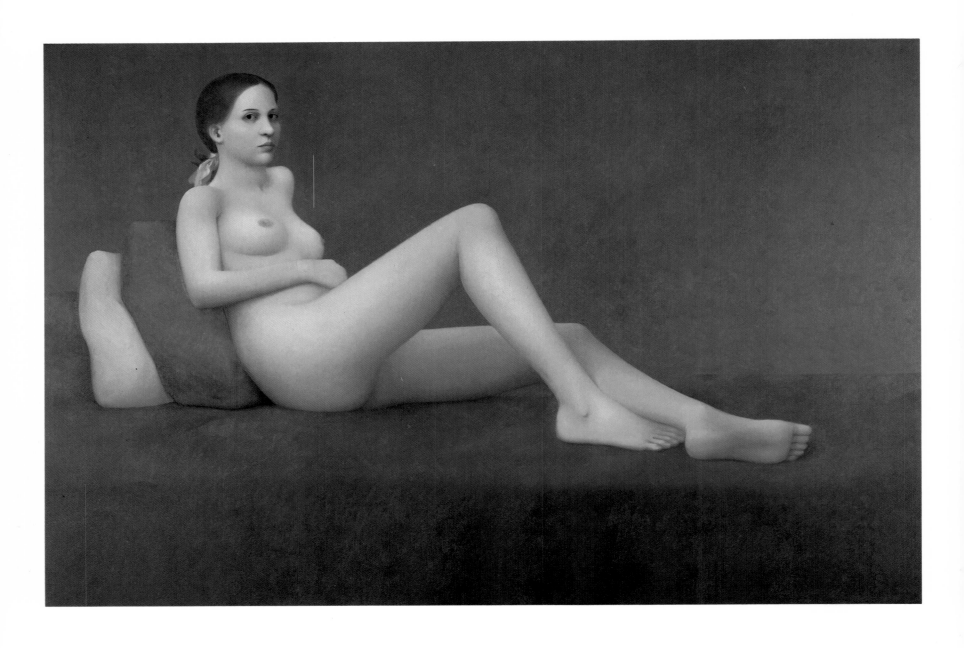

N
1964. Oil on canvas, 48 × 72 in.
Collection of Whitney Museum of American Art.

MIGIANELLA STILL LIFE WITH TUREEN
1973. Oil on canvas, 45 × 57$\frac{1}{2}$ in.
Kronos Collection.

In those days every New York show usually got a write-up and a tiny reproduction, so I knew of Pollock, of de Kooning. They were just beginning to be known. De Kooning had just had his first show. But the people that I was looking at most were all more or less socially conscious painters, people like Joe Hirsch, Ben Shahn, Kunyoshi, the Soyers. There was a whole slew of them, half of whose names I've forgotten.

I decided to leave Kansas for a number of reasons. Mainly because I thought that I had gotten just about all I could get out of the school as far as painting went. Also because I was convinced that I wanted to be a painter and a midwestern university at that time was a very hard place in which to develop and be taken seriously. I wanted to get away from college life and so on, so I decided to try and go to art school on the East Coast. But then the Korean War started. I was 1A and my family had no money. My father had died when I was fifteen. I knew that I'd have to get a job in order to go away to school, and there were no jobs. So I volunteered for the draft and went off to Japan and later to Korea for several months. All through that time I never told the army that I had any interest in art, because I was afraid that I would be put to work designing signs and things like that. I hated that kind of work and would rather have done anything else. But while I was in the army I did a lot of my own work—I kept notebooks and I did a lot of drawings—and then after Korea, when I went back to Japan, I rented a small place near the camp and set up a studio there, where I worked when I had time.

I was discharged from the army in February of '53 and still had no money except for the GI Bill, which was helpful but didn't pay tuition. So I had to make some money. On the advice of a friend I went to Wichita, Kansas, and got a job working as a draftsman for a steel company. I worked there through the spring and summer of '53, and by the fall I had saved some money. I set off for New York without really knowing what I was going to do. Someone suggested that I go up to New Haven and see Albers, which I did. I didn't

think that I'd be too interested, but he was the only one of the teachers I had talked with who really looked at the work seriously. He tore it apart and then said, "I'll take you." I started school at Yale in '53.

Albers was the first person I had studied with who convinced me that he himself and his ideas were of the first order. I think it was the force of his personality more than his work. He had lived through and participated in a good deal of the history of modern art and had known some of the principal figures like Klee and Kandinsky. He could look at any kind of work and make sense of it, from his own particular bias, which I can't say always pleased me but which made me think more clearly and look at my work in a much closer, more demanding way. At Yale during that time the great heroes, because of Albers, were Kandinsky, Klee, and Mondrian, who had never interested me. Yet there was a lot of student interest in the New York painters, and that created tension. The New York school and the Bauhaus didn't go together very well. Still, Albers liked de Kooning's black-and-white work, and it was on that basis that he invited de Kooning to Yale to teach. Albers also liked Marca-Relli's work at that time, and I studied with him in 1954–55.

My painting in those days was all over the place, and it certainly wasn't very good. I was trying to use everything that I was learning, and it didn't work. I tried to use color as Albers stressed it in his color course, that is, color forming its own structure, rather than adhering to a form arrived at through drawing or some other means. The kind of color I use now, and the purpose I put it to, is very, very different. For example, Albers paid very little attention to a tonal scale—the lightness or darkness of a color. He always talked about color in terms of hue or ways in which the color asserted itself. And those terms don't really meet the needs of a figurative painter. So later I had to teach myself whatever I know about tone.

I was always a figurative painter. The so-called abstract paintings that I did had figurative underpinnings. For me the central problem was how to put a

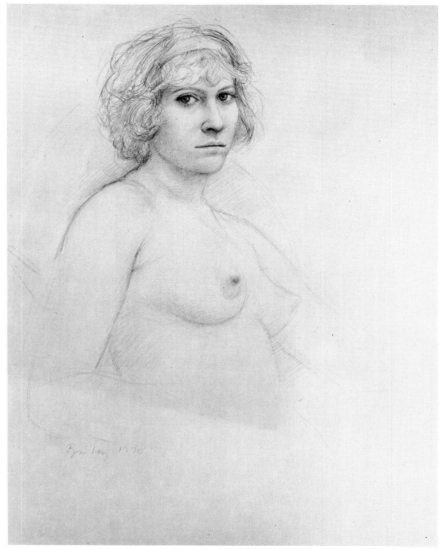

HEAD OF A GIRL (A PORTRAIT)
1970. Pencil, 14$^{15}/_{16}$ × 11$^{1}/_{4}$ in.
Collection of Yale University Art Gallery.

BUST OF FIGURE
1970. Pencil, 14$^{7}/_{8}$ × 11 in.
Private collection.

MIGIANELLA, EGGS, AND COFFEE POT
1975–76. Oil on canvas, $23\frac{1}{2} \times 31\frac{1}{2}$ in.
Private collection.

WILLIAM BAILEY

STILL LIFE WITH ROSE WALL AND COMPOTE
1977. Oil on canvas, 40 × 48 in. Collection of Hirshhorn
Museum and Sculpture Garden, Smithsonian Institution.

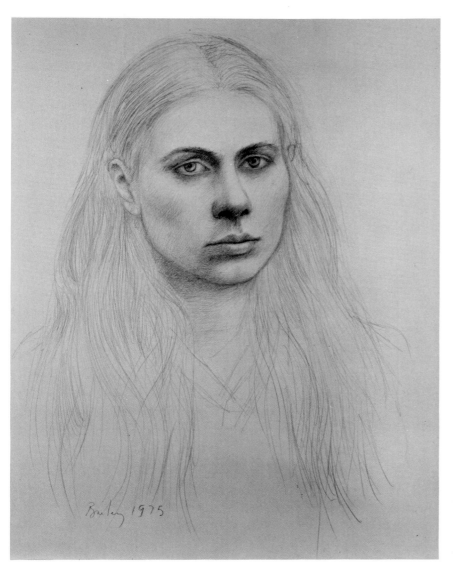

PORTRAIT OF DEE
1975. Pencil, 14 × 11 in.
Courtesy Robert Schoelkopf Gallery, Ltd.

figure into a modern painting. In modern painting, as I understood it, everything had a relationship to the picture plane that was obvious and primary and derived from cubism. That is, the illusion of sculpture was to be shunned. Of course, a flat Matisse figure can be sculptural because implicit in the articulation of the shape is a sense of its volume, but I didn't understand that then, or if I did understand it, it was only in the most intuitive way. That is, I wanted things that stood with great integrity on the surface as shapes and also stood for forms in space, forms in a pictorial space. And I didn't know how to do that. I was also concerned with the imperatives of the time: the gesture of the brush, a surface that reflected the act of painting, and perhaps most of all the improvisational aspect of painting.

Going to Yale was one of the most important changes in my career; the other was when I went to Southeast Asia in 1960. And that change had started earlier, but I didn't know it. I had been getting much closer to the issues of painting that have been my concern for the last twenty years—more than twenty years now. Still, before I went to Asia no form seemed inclusive enough for me, so I kept putting together disparate languages. In Picasso, whether you look at a cubist Picasso or you look at a classical, sculptural figure of Picasso's, or any Picasso, practically, they all seem to be made out of the same stuff. It's the stuff that Picasso has, knows, and controls, whether it's making a plane or a round form or whatever. He's in control of form. I didn't have that, that sense of stuff. So I was always going to style, to the look of a painting, and my painting seemed false. It all seemed too ephemeral. So I started doing sculpture in '59 or '60 with a friend in the basement of the art school after the students had gone. We hired a model and would do figures. We would do a figure and then tear it down and do another figure and tear it down. I made some little waxes from memory at that time. I did a lot of drawing and wasn't painting much at all.

Then an invitation from the State Department to visit Southeast Asia arrived. Not painting for three months and being out of the country, outside of Western culture, for that period of time had a sort of cleansing effect. I forgot all the things that I was supposed to be worried about. When we started back to the States we came through Europe and stopped in Athens and Rome and Paris and London. And I went right to certain things that I wanted to see. When I was in the Acropolis Museum in Athens, there was a room full of feet that had broken off sculptures—they were elegant and beautifully carved and seemed to have weight and meaning, tension and density. They were feet and at the same time they were extraordinary sculptural experiences. And it was from those Greek feet that I went to look at the Ingres *Odalisque* and *Bather of Valpinçon*—paintings like that.

When I got back to the States I started a painting of a figure in an empty room. It was very stylized, but still it was a figure in a measurable space, and it seemed terribly important to me—that painting really opened the door. My new paintings weren't very good, but the direction felt right. And really, from that point to this, my attitude about what painting is for me hasn't gone through any great changes, only subtle changes.

In that trip through Europe—and I'd been to Europe before, living in Rome in 1955–56—I was attracted not only to Ingres but to others who seemed to arrive at mystery through the clarity of their painting; it had seemed to me before that paintings drew their mystery from being ambiguous. I suddenly saw what I hadn't seen for a long time: I felt the greatest artistic freedom when dealing with a specific observable situation. I found that what had happened to me in trying to describe something was more abstract and carried more meaning than when I was simply trying to put something down that merely looked abstract. I found that I had been more literal when I wasn't working with the idea of making a figure in a real place. For example, today you see a lot of so-called abstract paintings that aren't abstract at all. They're very literal. The painter will put down a triangle, a circle, a piece of paint where it remains a triangle, a circle, a piece of paint in its exact measure.

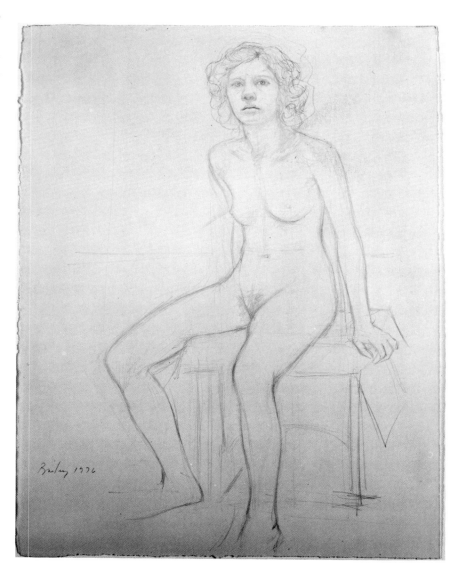

SEATED FIGURE
1976. Pencil, 14 × 11 in.
Courtesy of Robert Schoelkopf Gallery, Ltd.

GRECIAN STILL LIFE
1978. Oil on canvas, 42 × 50 in.
Collection of Edmund Pillsbury, Fort Worth.

FRATTA STILL LIFE
1978. Oil on canvas, 45 × 58 in.
Private collection, New York.

YOUNG GIRL WITH BRAID
1976. Pencil, 14 × 11 in.
Collection of Mr. and Mrs. Richard Kaplin,
Toledo, Ohio.

SEATED FIGURE
1976. Pencil, 14½ × 11 in.
Private collection.

I have been going to Italy part of every year for the past ten years. We have an old farmhouse in the hills north of Perugia. I think that my Italian paintings are more luminous and perhaps more volumetric than paintings done here, and that the proportions and the arrangement of things in them has much more to do with what I've absorbed from Italian town architecture. But again, it's not a conscious thing. I can look back on a painting and say, "This looks like it was done in New Haven, this looks like it was done in Italy." For example, I called one painting *Still Life Monterchi* because its colors reminded me of Monterchi, a town that looks like it comes right out of a Piero della Francesca, and is in fact the town that his mother came from. It is all greenish-bluish grays and pinks and ochers, unlike Umbrian towns, which are for the most part ochers and sienas. The *Madonna del Parto* is in Monterchi, and I often stop to see it on the way to Arezzo. So the title is based on association. All of my titles are more or less associations.

Neil Welliver once said something very good: When someone asked him what he did, he said, "I'm an avant-garde painter." Now Neil didn't mean that he was working within the conventions of avant-garde art. What he was saying was that he was finding values that were leading the way to something else. And in the early sixties I think that's the way a lot of us felt who had moved from modernist orthodoxies toward other values that we viewed as being modern and true to our experiences.

STILL LIFE
1977. Pencil, 13 × 21 in.
Collection of Dr. Murray D. List, New York.

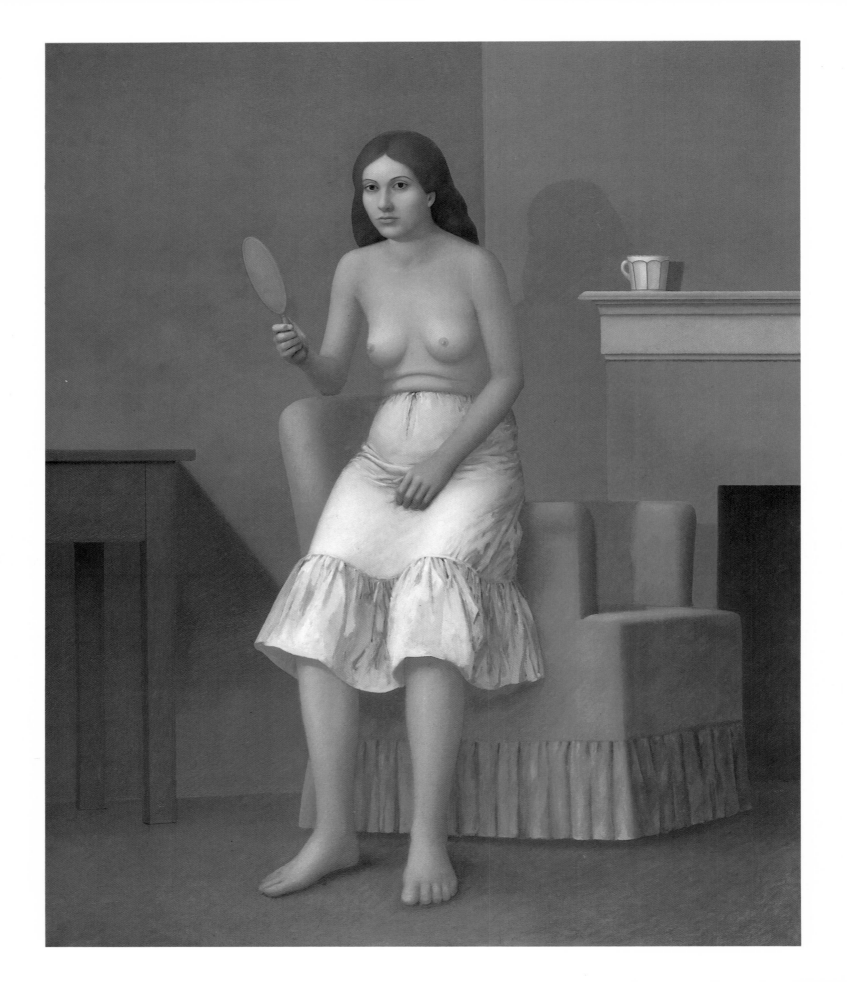

AGOSTINA
1978. Oil on canvas, 63¾ × 51½ in.
Kronos Collection.

GIRL WITH NECKLACE
1977. Pencil on paper, 11 × 14 in.
Collection of Daniel and Jeanne Halpern.

SEATED FIGURE
1978. Pencil, 11 × 14 in.
Private collection, New York.

WILLIAM BAILEY

PORTRAIT OF S
1980. Oil on canvas, 50 × 40 in.
Collection of University of Virginia Art Museum,
Charlottesville.

STILL LIFE—MONTERCHI
1981. Oil on canvas, 38 × 51 in.
Collection of Donald B. Marron.

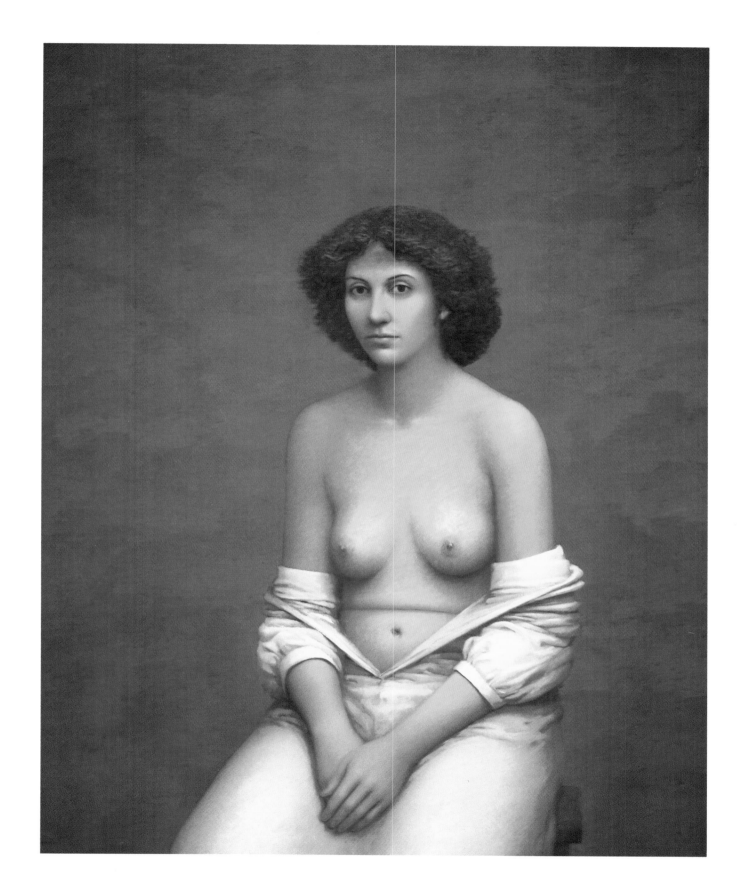

WILLIAM BAILEY

31

RECLINING FIGURE
1981. Pencil on paper, 30 × 22 in.
Collection of Mr. and Mrs. Stan Scholsohn, Connecticut.

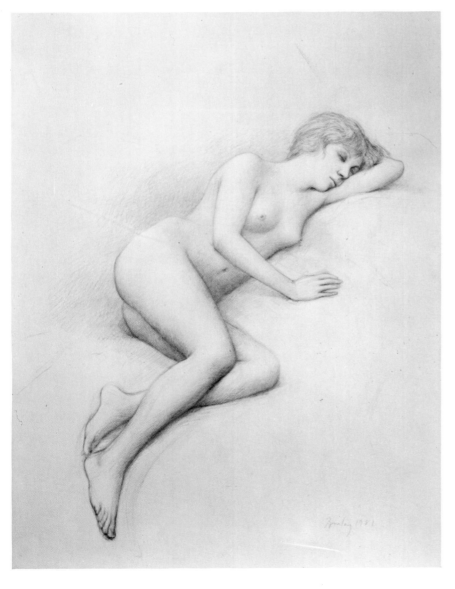

I think that every painter is finally self-taught. Partly, you teach yourself by looking at great things. Of course, as a student you rely on people with more experience, whose eyes are more acute than your own, to see how a painting works visually, and you learn something about materials, but those things in themselves don't teach you to be a painter. You teach yourself what must be learned. But you can do this only after discovering what is essential to your own vision.

I've often been questioned about the objects that appear in my still-life paintings. The reason I select these objects is because they are the kinds of things that I've always had around me, the kinds of objects I like. They are things that I look at out of the corner of my eye, whether in the kitchen or some other place in the house, so they have been convenient in that way. Another reason is that I don't want objects that seem to require a particular context, either historical or social. A realist would insist upon a contemporary context and meaning, whereas for me they have a metaphorical existence.

That's why I prefer the term *figurative* in describing my work. The word has a double meaning that reflects my concerns. One meaning has to do with painting figures or objects; the other is more literary, having to do with the metaphorical rather than literal character of what is painted. I think of my still lifes in architectural terms. My paintings are like imagined towns, not real ones. They are places for me, painting places. If there is idealism in my painting, it has more to do with a painting ideal than an ideal subject. I rarely ever think about the objects as being things that can be picked up or set down, least of all as things that can be used. My appropriation of these objects reflects formal concerns, with an expressive intention but not necessarily having to do with expressing anything that's peculiar to the objects themselves. More likely, they express something peculiar to me.

MERCATALE STILL LIFE
1981. Oil and wax on canvas, 30 × 40 in.
Collection, The Museum of Modern Art, New York.

STILL LIFE—PIAZZA FORTEBRACCIO
1981. Oil on canvas, 51 × 38 in.
Collection of Graham Gund.

WILLIAM BAILEY

When you look at something and say, "This has a very beautiful proportion," why do you say that? You say that because you have a certain normative vision for a form, how high a church steeple should be, for instance. Where does that measure come from? If you make a short one or a tall one, either one could be wrong or right. The reasons for its being wrong or right have entirely to do with some ineffable sense of measure, the appropriateness of a certain proportion. I alter the proportions of the objects that I use according to the needs of the painting. Things will be fat and short in one painting that are tall and slender in another. So objects are always used for their role in the painting rather than for themselves. The manipulation of perspective has a lot to do with scale. One visual paradox evident in my paintings which has nothing to do with realism is that the still life objects seem to be painted from up close and yet the whole still life seems to be viewed from a distance.

I draw from models and recently I've felt the need to paint directly from the model, which really means that I start with the model in a pose, and take off from there. I don't paint all the way through, looking at the model. Usually the painting is extended far beyond my time with the model. In fact, I do most of the painting away from the model. As a result, the painting usually loses one quality in favor of another.

In the case of the *Portrait of S.*, I worked on the painting over a period of two years. It was very hard to get it working together, that is, to get arms to go through the sleeves and to keep that white thing that she's wearing—which I wanted to make into a kind of nightdress—from being merely drapery. And there was a problem with trying to keep something that I liked about the luminosity of the breasts in relation to the face, in relation to the lap. And then qualities that you just can't talk about—the particular presence of that person.

I have an anxiety about the figure paintngs, and I find that this influences the work. It is hard to describe, but the anxiety I am talking about has to do with the nature of my relationship to the imagined figure and place. The figure takes on a reality for me and embodies many contradictions. I am forced to make changes, trying to get something right—but I can never say exactly what that thing is that will make the painting seem right to me. Some people find that my figures are like pots and cups and bowls. I've never felt that the figure or still-life paintings lack life—only that they are still and silent. The figure is more resistant to one's will or imagination. Just as people are more resistant than things to manipulation.

If I had lived in a time of shared myths and historical truths, as painters did in the past, I might have had reason to compose groups of figures instead of bowls and jars on a tabletop. For now, my interest in the human figure is focused upon an individual presence that I can begin to understand and believe in.

Recently, contemporary figurative painters have tried to revive the narrative in painting. I admire some of them for their courage and skill, but the narrative paintings they've produced haven't been convincing—the subjects seems self-conscious—either overly anecdotal or arcane. For me, a narrative would have to be completely assimilated into the formal language of painting before I could use it in a way that would allow me the artistic freedom, honesty, and authority I need. Perhaps I'm really an abstract painter after all.

STILL LIFE—PIAZZA BOLOGNA
1982. Pencil, 22 × 15¾ in.
Private collection, Boston.

WILLIAM BAILEY

STILL LIFE—UMBERTIDE
1981. Oil on canvas, 24 × 20 in.
Private collection.

STILL LIFE—CITTA DI CASTELLO
1980. Oil on canvas, 46½ × 35 in.
Private collection, New York.

WILLIAM BAILEY

Jack Beal

I had a lot of trouble with ear infections when I was a kid, so my mother tried to invent different ways for me to amuse myself because I was laid up in bed so much. She got me to read or she would read to me, but she also encouraged me to draw. So I drew a lot. Later, because of my parents' problems, I lived in orphanages and foster homes, and quite often, because I was never accepted in those places, I would draw. It was something I could do better than anybody else. I would draw either to attract attention or to relieve some of the pressure on me.

I always received compliments for the work I did, but I never thought of painting seriously as a profession until after I'd been in college for a couple of years and I had an art teacher there whose first piece of advice was to leave college and go to a good art school. And her second piece of advice was to go to the Art Institute of Chicago, which was the best in the country at that time. So in the autumn of 1953 I started at the Art Institute of Chicago, one of the biggest turning points of my life, because all of a sudden within a couple of weeks I was totally devoted to the notion of art as a career and began to see it as something that I could do and something that I could excel at.

I left art school in 1956 having painted nothing but nonfigurative paintings for probably the last year and a half of my time there; then for the next five years I primarily painted nonfiguratively, although I always drew figuratively. At that time I thought the only serious art that could be made was nonfigurative. Also, realist art itself is an embarrassment to those folks who have built up a vested interest in modernism as a supposedly logical evolution; the fact that the smallest area of a realist painting can have more content and more aesthetic possibilities than the entire surface of most huge modern works is obviously disturbing to them.

That was a period when, like most everybody else in my generation, I worshipped Picasso above all. But I saw him as distant and beyond my reach, so I tried most to emulate the people with whom I could more closely identify—people like de Kooning and Gorky. Then, some years after my wife, Sondra, and I moved to New York, something happened that impressed me. Quite often when I finished painting at the end of the day—sometimes it'd be three or four o'clock in the morning—I'd go out in the streets and take a walk to clear my head before I went to sleep. One night I was

NUDE WITH PATTERNED PANEL
1966. Oil on canvas, 70 × 76 in.
Collection of John and Mable Ringling Museum of Art, Sarasota, Florida.

PORTRAIT OF THE DOYLES
1971. Oil on canvas, 78 × 58 in.
Private collection.

STILL LIFE WITH SELF-PORTRAIT
1974. Oil on canvas, 29 × 28 in.
Valparaiso University Art Collections,
Valparaiso, Indiana.

walking up University Place and I saw one of my heroes drunk in the gutter and I looked at him and I was so shocked that I could not even help him up. I think I realized then that perhaps what those painters were doing had more to do with my parents' generation than with my own. It was shortly after that encounter that I began to paint figuratively. I was already feeling dissatisfied with the kind of work that I was doing, because it was not fulfilling me in the way that I had been taught that art could fulfill me.

One of the things I've always tried to do is to remember what brought me into art in the first place, what those first notions were, those first cravings, those first loves and desires. The first person that I can remember really admiring was a fellow named Ben Stahl. He was part of the Famous Artists School in Westport, Connecticut, and he was best known for painting frowsy nudes that were used on the covers of John Steinbeck paperback novels. They were somewhat impressionistic and very alluring. It was that kind of work that drew me in the first place. So I keep trying to go back to that. Braque made a statement one time about eliminating preconceptions in your work because if you could get into a painting and eliminate all preconceptions, then you would find yourself realizing the ambitions of your earliest youth. And I thought that was such a lovely statement because artists don't talk about that generally, about what they used to be and how they got to where they are. I see so much of art these days as done by members of a private club. Now I think about making paintings for the people who are like I was when I was young. And making paintings specifically for me.

It took me six years of total immersion in modernism and finally a disenchantment with it to get me back to realism again. What happened was that in the summer of 1962, Sondra and I and a couple who were friends of ours rented a house in upstate New York. I'd been wasting my time for several years painting without believing in what I was doing. I really felt lost and did a lot of things, almost trying to prevent myself from painting. For instance, a friend of mine and I bought a racing car together, and I was the full-time mechanic on that, so when we went away in the summer of '62 I sort of thought of it as a last chance: I was going to give art one more try and see if I could find something that I could be totally immersed in.

I decided that what I wanted to do was to make my paintings more natural; get more natural form and color into them. When we got out to the country, and without intending to do so, without having any plan in mind, I started painting from nature, from what was in front of me. And before I knew it, I was painting all day long every day. I fell in love with art all over again. And I didn't even know that that was possible. I started making paintings that felt like they were mine. For the first time I felt that I had my feet under me. The paintings had almost everything in them, or as much in them as I was able to put of what I had learned. Although they owed enormous debts to a number of other people, the debts were largely repaid in the pictures. That is, I was making personal statements about what I was seeing in front of me. I was reacting to what I saw in front of me instinctively rather than just intellectually, as before. I was able to merge my learning with the sensations that were bombarding me. I had learned that everything done in modernism could be used in making pictures from life. My generation was characterized by a desire to "try everything—do it all." When I found a way to paint that included everything and excluded no possibilities, I dove in headfirst. I was squeezing paint all over the brushes, slapping it onto the canvas, like the *Sondra in the Bathing Suit* that I made in Maryland in 1963.

By 1965, when I had my first show, my color had been played down quite a bit. I was trying to arrive at a more realistic appraisal of what I was looking at. So, since we were living in a dark New York loft, the paintings became darker and the color was not as high in the first couple of shows that I had. But I began to miss that lush color that I'd grown to love, and so I began, say, by 1967, wanting to pump color back into the paintings, to see if I couldn't merge my love of color

SONDRA IN THE BATHING SUIT
1963. Oil on canvas, 51 × 55 in.
Collection of the artist.

DANAË II
1972. Oil on canvas, 68 × 68 in.
Collection of the Whitney Museum of American Art, New York.

NUDE ON RED SOFA
1973–74. Oil on canvas, 67 × 72 in.
Private collection.

PORTRAIT OF SYDNEY AND FRANCES LEWIS
1975. Oil on canvas, 72 × 78 in.
Collection of Washington and Lee University,
Lexington, Virginia.

with my desire to make realistic paintings. And a funny thing happened en route; the love of color sort of took charge of the paintings and submerged the realism. And that continued until about 1970.

In 1970 we made a trip west, drove to the West Coast, drove through Utah and New Mexico and Arizona and saw all that great natural color that exists out there, as opposed to the natural color in the east: green. And I came back to New York and made the painting with Jane and Tom Doyle, which was again another big turning point in my life because I was able finally to merge my love of color with the kind of realism that I had wanted to paint. Since 1970 I think that the marriage between my love of color and my love of nature has been a better marriage.

I've always been a student of art and of art history. I'm constantly making discoveries about aesthetics. And I felt the need quite often to apply those discoveries in my own work. I did a series once of paintings of a single table, wanting to explore that table in as many ways as possible in terms of space, composition, color, etc. I ended up making seventeen paintings of this one table, which was seen then, and I'm sure would be in retrospect, as a very eccentric act on my part. But it was something that I needed to do to clarify certain issues in my head. I'm not a person who can visualize something without having done it. I've sometimes said that I've had scholarships all my life, because a great many of my paintings have been experimental and collectors have been good enough to buy them and support me in my education. The only way I can really learn anything is by doing it myself. I can listen, I can study, I can discuss with other people, but finally I have to do it to find out whether it's good or not.

I love to see how other people have done things to see if I can do them that way or similarly or maybe differently. Besides color, I'm interested in composition—pictorial composition—which is something that I feel has not been stressed in teaching. There are a number of books on the subject, most of which really don't deal with the issue at all. It's something that cannot be taught easily. I know that in music and in writing there are composition classes, but in art schools there are very few classes in composition. I love trying to create dynamic compositions. I work in sketchbooks, almost abstractly, figuring out how to put different masses together to make pictures exciting. I had an art history teacher named Kathleen Blackshear, and every week she had us bring in analytical drawings of a work of art done most basically from six points of view. First, second, and third dimension, value, color, and texture. I have a somewhat scientific, analytical bent and I like to understand things thoroughly, so that was a very exciting process for me. Nobody had ever taught me anything like that before. And it has been carried forward in my work.

My color masters, if I may say, were Braque and Bonnard, and I loved the way that they used color. I think that there have been very few great colorists in modernism, and I think they were two great colorists.

I don't think modernist painters generally have attempted to reach a broad audience. When I was an abstract painter I used to share the fantasy that here we were painting toward a brave new world and that everybody would sooner or later be able to understand what we were doing. But that fantasy has slowly died in me because I think such work finally makes untrained or uneducated people feel ignorant and then hostile. And if art is going to do that then art is going to drive away its audience. You see, I don't think that there's anything that's been done in modernist abstraction that can't be done in a realist painting. In other words, I think that realism can embody all the conceptualism, all the minimalism, all the aesthetics that modernism has embodied, plus a great deal more. And in the process, a painting can be made that has something for the most highly trained intellectual viewer as well as the least trained. A motto that I have now for myself is somewhat cryptic, somewhat simplistic: "Make art like life, make life like art."

I have learned at least as much of how to live better in this world, at least as much about beauty, at least as much about dealing with other human beings, from works of art as I have from life itself. And so I want to

SELF-PORTRAIT WITH CAP AND LENSES
1982. Pastel on paper, 23½ × 20 in.
Collection of Dr. Eugene A. Solow.

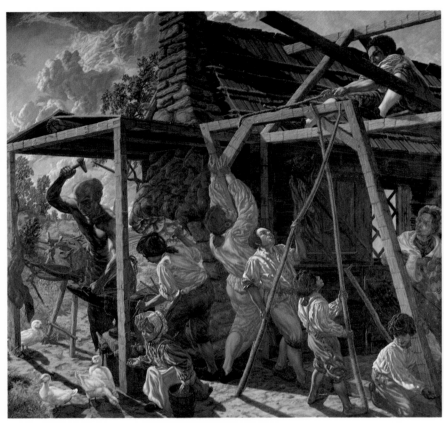

THE HISTORY OF LABOR IN AMERICA
1975–76. Four oil on canvas paintings, each 12 × 12 ft.

17th-Century ''Colonization,''
18th-Century ''Settlement,''
19th-Century ''Industry,''
20th-Century ''Technology.''

General Services Administration,
United States Department of Labor.

make art that contributes to the tradition. I have learned from John Donne and William Shakespeare and from Caravaggio things that I could not have learned anywhere else. For example, in *King Lear* we learn that people are much more perceptive about the problems of others than their own problems, and that the faults we find most obvious in others are generally faults in our own characters, and most often those we fail to recognize. I've learned from life, also, but there are times when the great artist can show something from life that we ought all to have been able to see clearly but were not able to see.

Quite often there are things that I want to say in a painting that if said too simply will end up looking corny and so I have to find a way to say them without being blatant. As a result, I've been called one of the most defamatory things that an artist can be called in our day, a "social realist," which is okay with me. In my painting *The Harvest* I wanted to celebrate the two people who mean most to me, Sondra and the artist Dana Van Horn, and their hard work—but I did not want to make a bucolic Pollyanna picture. So they look at you with serious eyes, interrupted in their work, ready to get back to gathering the harvest.

You see, one of the things that amuses me is that people talk about realism as though it were something invented by Gustave Courbet in the middle of the nineteenth century in France. Well, how do they feel about the entire Renaissance, the seventeenth century in Holland and in France, and all the great eighteenth- and nineteenth-century painters before Courbet? They were also realist painters, and many of them were social realist painters. They had a social impulse and felt a social responsibility and made paintings about that. Alfred Leslie has said it more beautifully, more succinctly than I've been able to say it. He said he wanted to make paintings to influence the conduct of others. And I feel very much that way, because I feel I have the responsibility to repay what I have been given. I've learned from so many other people, I need to be able to pass that on. Trying to imitate or compete with science, modernism took so much out of art—so-

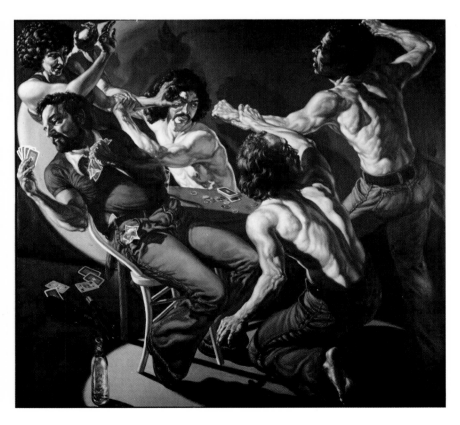

PRUDENCE, AVARICE, LUST, JUSTICE, ANGER
1977–78. Oil on canvas, 72 × 78 in.
University of Virginia Art Museum, Charlottesville.

cial impulses and message art became taboo. But it puzzles me that in the arts, where freedom is so cherished, painters should be roundly chastised for doing what artists did for thousands of years and what writers do as a matter of course—combine message with aesthetics. Of course, it is more of a challenge and it does make the work more difficult, but I'd give up painting before abandoning this ambition.

I don't think I realized it at the time, but during the process of making the murals for the Department of Labor I did spend some time figuring out what the impetus was, because first of all two people whose opinions I respect, my wife and my dealer, tried very gently to dissuade me from taking on that job, because they knew that it was going to drive me crazy—and they were right. But I wanted to make a statement that drew from the world and gave back to the world in equal proportion, because I depend on other people all the time. Supermarket clerks, engineers who make our electricity, people who pave the highways, etc. I wanted to be able to give something back to them.

I try to imagine the life on the canvas as being as real as the life off the canvas. I'm always a little hesitant about talking about this because I think one of these days I'm going to open up to somebody and they're going to call in the padded wagon and haul me away. I try to imagine that what's going on in there is a world that is as real as this world. I talk to the people in the painting while I'm painting them—I pretend that I'm walking into the canvas. There were times when we were working on the Labor murals, painting on the high scaffolding, that we got so deeply involved with the paintings that when we felt the need to grab on to something, we grabbed for something in the picture. So it's that kind of commitment that I mean.

There is right now a particular bias against message art. Just recently, in a talk at the Whitney, Hilton Kramer said something that illustrates that very clearly. It's been quoted to me three times now by people who seem to think that I ought to pay attention to it; something to the effect that meaningful subject matter never saved a bad picture. Well, you see, to be very harsh

HOPE, FAITH, CHARITY
1977–78. Oil on canvas, 72 × 72 in.
Private collection.

UNTITLED
1979. Pastel on gray paper, $47\frac{1}{2} \times 47\frac{1}{2}$ in.
Private collection, New York.

HARVEST
1979–80. Oil on canvas, 96 × 96 in.
Collection of Galerie Claude Bernard, Paris.

JACK BEAL
55

about this, as far as I'm concerned if a painting doesn't have meaningful subject matter it's a bad picture to begin with. I mean if you were to tell a seventeenth-century Dutchman that meaningful subject matter was not important he would have laughed you out of town. Frans Hals painted those warders of the old folks' home, drunk and disorderly and lounging around. To him, subject matter was meaningful, and he made it more so. We've gotten away from that partially because I think our time is such that appearance and style count for so much. If you're not properly dressed and don't behave properly you know you're going to be looked at askance. So most of us try to disguise our inner selves, these days, and I feel that life has been diminished in the process. Since I think that paintings can show our private needs and desires clearly, I have recently realized that perhaps the most intense emotion that a painter can engender in a viewer now is embarrassment. The most effective paintings that are being made are paintings that will embarrass other people, because we have become so overloaded—movies and television have so inured us to expression of every other emotion—that finally embarrassment is the only one that's left. By embarrassment I mean that the painter is touching on such private emotions that the person recognizes the feelings in him or herself and feels uncomfortable because of them. At the risk of being self-serving, I must mention that my *Virtues and Vices* series was received with embarrassed reactions to an extent that astonished me.

Most of what we see when we walk around is not very beautiful. The artist must be selective. He can't just look at nature randomly, find a great subject and make a great painting about it. There has to be a process of thought there, a conceptual process. All the different -isms that have been broken down in contemporary art into various art movements come into play until the artist selects the subject that is most meaningful for him at that time. And then I think it's natural that there be a transformation. And that transformation is more obvious in some artists' work than others. Some artists are relatively naturalistic—say, the Dutch painters. Other artists modify what they see in front of them to varying degrees. I've always been someone who modifies more than many of my contemporaries do, because I'm more interested in the total life experience and the total painting experience than I am in achieving some kind of visual verisimilitude, which can be captured magnificently by a photograph. But the realities of life are something else again. I mean, for example, when I have people pose for me I don't insist that they sit absolutely rock still. I like to catch them as they're moving, catch them in action, and that sometimes results in features not being placed exactly in the right relationship. But it has more to do with them as living human beings than it does with some insect-collection sort of thing.

My ambition to wed art and life is a terribly difficult one. I needn't bang my breast and feel sorry for myself, although I sometimes do, but I think it's the most exciting and most rewarding challenge. The opportunity is there for more people to become involved with the work. I don't want to see people awed by paintings. I'd rather see an ambitious problematical work than simplistic finished work, because I think that it's more like life. The quest for absolute perfection in art—which developed only when the modernists lowered the stakes by going reductive—has been very damaging to art. It limits imagination and ambition, pictorial and social. Obviously I try to finish my paintings, I try to arrive at some decent conclusion to them, but most often I end up abandoning pictures because I don't know what they need, what I need to do to make them better than they are. But I think it's worthwhile trying, reaching above your head, trying to do something more challenging, more exciting, and more like life.

UNTITLED LANDSCAPE (BARN AND TREES)
1978. Pen and ink wash, 18 × 21½ in.
Collection of Brooke and Carolyn Alexander.

STILL LIFE PAINTER
1978–79. Oil on canvas, 49¾ × 60 in.
The Toledo Museum of Art,
Toledo, Ohio.
© Toledo Museum of Art, 1979.

JACK BEAL

STILL LIFE WITH FRENCH EASEL
1982. Oil on canvas, 24 × 36 in.
Courtesy Allan Frumkin Gallery, New York.

Jane Freilicher

I got out of high school right after Pearl Harbor, and having just turned seventeen, I eloped with a jazz musician, an aspiring composer who doubled on trombone in the West Point Army Band. I lived a strange life near the post there. I remember painting on some discarded kettledrum heads during this period. When I resumed my education, I majored in art at Brooklyn College. I was very involved in listening to jazz and contemporary music and that's how I met Nell Blaine, who was married to a French horn player, and Larry Rivers, who played in a band with my husband and had never thought about painting but became interested in it through me and Nell. On Nell's advice, Larry and I both decided to study with Hans Hofmann.

Hofmann was a great connection, a bridge between traditional art and modern art as it was evolving. He had an inspiring heroic quality, a very strong Germanic aura, like a Wagnerian tenor crossed with Santa Claus, a real grandfather figure.

The school was very rigorous, the level of aspiration very high, and it was quite intimidating and awe-inspiring to a neophyte, which I was.

I remember receiving, after I'd been there a month or two, a negative criticism, and going home and crying. I was taken by surprise by how much I cared and at the same time was happy to realize how much it meant to me. I felt, after that point, that I had passed through some door of commitment, a very serious moment in my life. After a while when he felt your work was coming along Hofmann would cease to criticize and just go by your chair with a little nod or a pat. I studied with him for about a year. This was in the late forties. My marriage was over. I got a masters in art education at Columbia, in case I ever needed to get a job teaching.

I had my first show in 1952 at John Myer's Tibor de Nagy gallery. The art world was so different then. It was small, intimate. Everybody knew everybody else and nobody hoped to make money out of it because very few paintings were sold in those days. Looking back there seemed to be a sense of adventurousness, a playfulness that no longer exists.

The painters who first attracted me when I began to paint seriously were Matisse, Léger, Mondrian, and a bit later Bonnard, Vuillard. I guess everybody in my generation thought a lot about Cézanne, Picasso, and, for me, Bill de Kooning rather than Pollock.

STILL LIFE WITH CALENDULAS
1954–55. Oil on canvas, 65½ × 49½ in.
Collection of the artist.

CON EDISON
1970. Oil on canvas, 48 × 46 in.
Courtesy Fischbach Gallery.

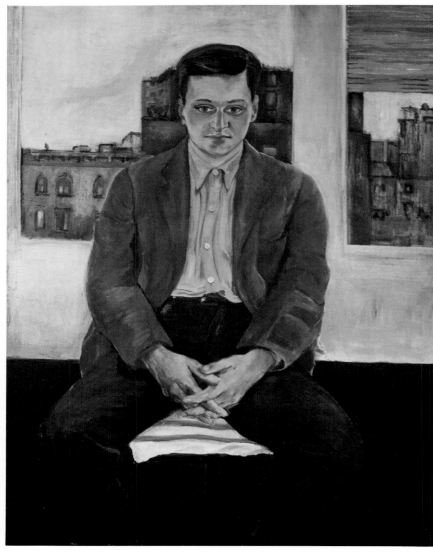

AFTER WATTEAU'S ''LE MEZZETIN''
1950. Oil on cardboard. 22½ × 30 in.

PORTRAIT OF JOHN ASHBERY
ca. 1953–54. Oil on canvas, 56 × 60 in.

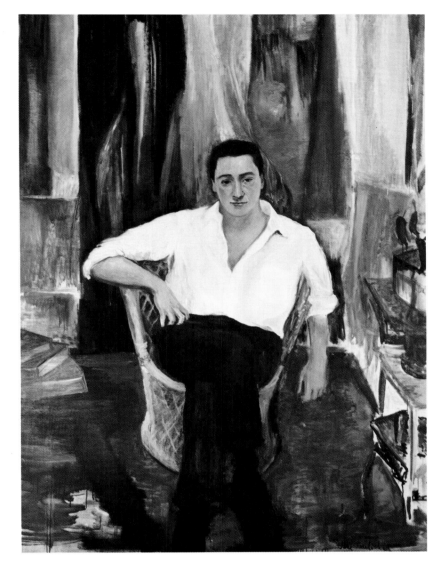

PORTRAIT OF ARNOLD WEINSTEIN
1958. Oil on canvas, 82 × 58½ in.
Collection of the artist.

WOMAN IN A PHOTOGRAPH (SELF PORTRAIT)
1963. Oil on canvas, 40 × 32 in.
Collection Stratford College, Stratford, Connecticut.

NUDE ON A GREEN BLANKET
1967. Oil on canvas, 25 × 30 in.
Collection of the artist.

LOAVES AND FISHES
1972. Oil on canvas, 42 × 38 in.
Collection of Dr. Stanley and Sophia Schachter.

JANE FREILICHER

In 1957 I married Joe Hazan and we began spending summers in Watermill in eastern Long Island. We built a house and I've painted the views that I see out of my studio windows since the early sixties.

I like being near the ocean. The particular landscape around my studio is so flat and open—the sky out there seems to be endless. You feel you're in a universe of light, you feel the convexity of the earth, the horizons curving down at the periphery.

I'm sort of depressed by mountains and lonely vast vistas. I like landscape on a human rather than a sublime scale. I enjoy the intimation of a human touch in the landscape as opposed to many painters who want to feel that man has never put his mark on it. I like to include something man-made like a house or maybe the line of a sailboat moored across the bay which will somehow seem very important to me. In the painting called *The Green Squirearchy*—a phrase that appears in a poem by John Ashbery, which caught my fancy, one of my few literary titles—a man in a boat suddenly appeared on the creek as I was finishing the painting. The man was there to put up a duck blind, which only happens once a year. I felt impelled to quickly notate it in the painting; he was only there a very few minutes. The inclusion of that boat seemed to resolve the painting like a punctuation mark at the end of a sentence.

It's difficult to explain what I am trying to do in my paintings because in a way it's a secret even from myself. To paraphrase something that Braque said: It's the mystery in the painting that is the valid part. I try to retain a kind of sensation of flux, of having just looked at something and found it beautiful, without having analyzed why it was so. How to capture the poetry of the moment and yet make it stick. To give it gravity and weight without losing the spontaneity and informality. You can't do it by the diligent rendering of the world of objects and yet you don't want it to look "once over lightly." You can never really get what's out there so you have to create an equivalent world in the painting not just by a literal transcription of details. You start accumulating marks on the canvas which in turn ignite their own sparks and sometimes you have to give up your original impetus and go where the painting leads you.

There's an analogy to cooking. You start with a lot of different ingredients but once you've mixed them together you have something new. You can't get back to the original elements. You just have to keep tasting and adjusting them in their relation to each other. There's a risk involved and an element of surprise.

I tend to start a painting by plunging in headlong. I like to start at a high energy level rather than dissipating it in plans and sketches, so I guess in a way I'm an "action" painter. I'll often put something down right smack in the middle of the canvas, a cut of horizon, of whatever, and then having created an obstacle, work like crazy, shifting, altering, inventing, taking out and putting in, willing the picture into being. The final result of all that struggle is the picture, which may not in the least reveal the turmoil that went into its making.

Painting landscapes presents all sorts of challenges. For one thing, as the song goes "when the blue of sky meets the gold of the day," you've already got a big problem. How to relate and differentiate between the blue of sky and water and all those greens, all that air and light, keep a feeling for the glory of nature and yet not sink into a miasma of gorgeousness and sentimentality.

I know that I use the elements of the window on the view and the structure of the studio interior to impose some control on a landscape that is very flat and without much incident, tending to run off the canvas at both ends. Painting the outside from the inside through a window adds another dimension and raises questions of the relation of the painter to the landscape.

NUDE WITH RAISED ARMS
1966. Oil on canvas, 27 × 28 in.
Collection of the artist.

BACKGAMMON
1975. Oil on canvas, 38 × 44 in. Collection of Utah Museum
of Fine Arts, University of Utah, Salt Lake City.

EDGE OF GARDEN PAINTED OUTDOORS
1976. Oil on canvas, 65 × 46 in.
Collection of Dr. and Mrs. Harold Ehrlich.

JANE FREILICHER

70

THE MALLOW GATHERERS
1958. Oil on canvas, 76 × 77 in.
Collection of the artist.

Adding a particular practical difficulty for me is the fact that this landscape around my studio that I've been painting for so long has been sold to a developer. Last year when they first started digging out there, going back and forth in front of the studio with bulldozers, the noise and sense of violation drove me nuts. One day I caught myself in a mirror while I was painting, feeling desperate with a bunch of brushes in my hand, so I included myself in the painting, glaring back out the canvas, perhaps looking for some kind of sympathy while this ditch was being created. A bulldozer and three men having a coffee break were in the field. At the same time that I hated it, I realized there was something rather beautiful about it, and I got interested in the opportunity to paint some hillocks of freshly turned earth and the colors of the machine and the men. (The painting is called *Changing Scene.*)

Another painting called *Landscape, July 1981* was the

last in a series of one particular view. As I was painting it, the barn that I had painted over and over for the last twenty years seemed to change its appearance every day and then one day it simply wasn't there anymore. It had been cut in half and carried away. A friend called and said, "That barn in your field—I saw it on the Montauk Highway." It had been sold and was being carried away to its new location. My mood was very deliberate while I finished that painting, very elegaic. But this year I've painted the landscape again in its altered form.

When I came out to the studio last summer the developers had made a serious engineering error. They had scraped off too much topsoil and the heavy spring rains had created a pond, really a huge ditch. So I decided to paint this new-found body of water and also to include a still life with certain flowers that are a kind of talisman for me because I seem to have luck both growing them and painting them. So on this one morning I cut some poppies and peonies as their season was nearly over. I cut them in the bud and put them in the refrigerator to slow down their opening.

TELEPHONE POLES
1962. Charcoal pencil, 5½ × 8 in.
Collection of the artist.

IN BROAD DAYLIGHT
1979. Oil on canvas, 70 × 90 in.
Collection of Marion Koogler McNary Art Institute,
San Antonio, Texas.

FLOWERS AND STRAWBERRIES
1980. Oil on canvas, 50 × 47 in.
Collection of Mr. and Mrs. Henri Doll.

However, I was working on another painting and couldn't get around to them. My daughter kept opening the refrigerator and saying, "Please get rid of these flowers. Every time I look for something to eat I find them. You're never going to paint them."

So finally I had to face the fact that the flowers weren't going to survive much longer. I took them out of the refrigerator and plunked them down on the table in my studio in front of the window on the pond. It was a very bright, hot time of year and I knew they were going to die within twenty-four hours, which they did. So I painted them very rapidly, trying not to think too much about the problems I was creating for myself. (Actually that's the way I seem to start a painting—by doing something a little improvident.) The flowers were against the light, way off to one side of the canvas and the heat was withering them as I painted. I got them down very fast and then went on to the rest of the painting. I had some notion of where the bottom on the window ledge and the horizon would be. I put in the sky very blue. The painting looked sort of raw. I came to realize that the sky wasn't blue at all and overpainted a sort of grayish-pinkish haze since the light was coming from overhead, hence the title, *Light from Above.* But then the pond looked like a slice in the middle of the picture and I realized that I had been ignoring a huge population of birds that had little by little settled into this new watering hole. I painted them in and they seemed to take care of the picture. All this illustrates the way one capitalizes on some unforeseen or unplanned circumstance.

Toward the end of the summer I get tired of doing landscapes. I feel a "landscape glut." I've got green up to my ears and it's good to get away from it. I enjoy getting back to the city where there's another dominant tonality: softer colors and sharper light.

I imagine the way one works, one's choices and inclinations, are to a large extent predetermined. I believe the notion that biology is destiny is true, not in the narrow sense to which feminists object, but in a broader way. I think it's almost a genetic thing—the way your hand moves, what your metabolism is, how compulsive you are, how anxious or driven, what kinds of forms and colors attract you, whether you are neat or messy. I know my basic impulse is really to mess around with paint and make something out of it. That primitive pleasure is the basis of my work, and I don't want to lose it. I think that nowadays a lot of painting looks terribly far away from any primal impulse to paint.

Landscape and still life are probably metaphors for the human figure, and your own sense of your body is probably lurking on a subliminal level. Sometimes I think I'm drawn to painting a rather gentle, passive landscape or the soft form of flowers and draperies which might in some way be an analog of a recumbent female figure to give the lie to the actual sense of tension and anxiety that is usually present while I'm painting.

Every serious artist is always straining against limits. You go on, you try something else, but it's still you. Sometimes I am rather sad about that because I feel, "Oh, I never did paint that picture with five hundred people in it and, you know, *Liberty Leading the Revolution.*" But with experience you also have to learn to understand your own nature and accept it and make the most of it because not only are you stuck with it but it is what makes you unique.

When I was starting out, figurative painting was held in deep contempt, now it's come back into fashion. One was warned years ago to "make it new," now I can hear a demand to "make it real." But what is real and what is new? Whatever they are, it seems to me that painting is about something else.

SELF-PORTRAIT IN A MIRROR
1971. Oil on canvas, 38 × 42 in.
Collection of National Academy of Design, New York.

JANE FREILICHER

FISH, ONIONS, FLOWERS, AND PHOTO
1981. Oil on canvas, 40 × 40 in.
Private collection.

CHANGING SCENE
1981. Oil on canvas, 52 × 64 in.
Courtesy Fischbach Gallery.

BONED STRIPED BASS
1973. Oil on canvas, 20 × 22 in.
Collection of Mr. and Mrs. Robert Goldfein.

ONE CAT, TWO FISH (HOMAGE TO SUKI)
1974. Oil on canvas, 47 × 50 in.
Collection of Lois E. Dickson.

STILL LIFE, OPALESCENT VASE
1982–83. Oil on canvas, 32 × 40 in.
Collection of Dr. and Mrs. Harold Ehrlich.

WHEN IT SNOWED IN APRIL
1982. Oil on canvas, 47 × 50 in.
Courtesy Fischbach Gallery.

JANE FREILICHER

BURNETT'S BARN PASTEL
1978. Pastel, 26½ × 34½ in.
Collection of Dr. and Mrs. Richardson Davidson.

FLOWERING CHERRY PASTEL I
1978. Pastel, 34¼ × 26½ in.
Collection of Mr. and Mrs. J. Meisel.

THE GREEN SQUIREARCHY
1981. Oil on canvas, 85 × 76 in.
Collection of Rahr-West Museum, Manotowoc, Wisconsin.

SIESTA
1982. Oil on canvas, 76 × 76 in.
Courtesy Fischbach Gallery.

JANE FREILICHER

Philip Pearlstein

The whole progress of my painting has been circular in that what I am doing now is probably closer to what I started out doing in high school. There was an active art program at the high school I went to in Pittsburgh and I painted very much in the style of Reginald Marsh—perhaps a little denser. I worked in oils and watercolors, painting very elaborate compositions: carousels, amusement-park scenes, and social comment-type paintings. It was still the time of the Great Depression.

In 1942, before my nineteenth birthday, after one year at Carnegie Tech, I was drafted. I spent a year in Florida at a training center doing charts and diagrams, perspective drawings of machine guns that were then reproduced by silk screen. It really was a terrific apprenticeship, because I was working with commercial artists.

During the time I spent in Florida, I did a whole series of watercolors that were complicated compositions of military training scenes, almost in the style of Cézanne's big *Bathers* but drawn in a tighter Renaissance-like manner. When I got to Italy I carried a small sketchbook with me and made very complex little drawings, such as scenes of soldiers standing on railroad station platforms with begging kids coming up to them, still in a Reginald Marsh–like style. Later on, when I could, I started doing the watercolors again. I guess I was thinking in terms of a postwar career as an illustrator, though the scenes I did were of everyday life in the army in Rome. I was very self-conscious about making finished works that would perhaps hold up as a portfolio to take around after the war. But when I got back to Pittsburgh, I decided to finish college first. So I went back to Carnegie Tech for three more years. I worked in all kinds of styles, flirted with abstraction, and forgot about being so representational. My work was mainly figurative but kept going off into different kinds of symbolist-related styles. You can see the influences all the way from van Gogh to Picasso and Matisse, and a lot of the postimpressionists.

When I came to New York I got a job doing catalogs for American Standard Sanitary. The people there would get together all the stuff for, say, a hospital-equipment catalog. I would organize it and draw up the rough sketches, and the guy I worked for would design the pages. My own paintings at this time were very eccentric and didn't fit into any category easily.

PORTRAIT OF AL HELD AND SYLVIA STONE
1968. Oil on canvas, 66 × 72 in.
Private collection.

FEMALE MODEL IN ROBE SEATED ON PLATFORM ROCKER
1973. Oil on canvas, 72 × 60 in.
San Antonio Museum Association, San Antonio, Texas.

I can't relate them to any single master. They were an attempt to arrive at my own synthesis. But they were strange paintings, made up of what looked like large jigsaw-puzzle shapes, each painted in a different color and not necessarily fitted together. They gradually got somewhat clearer, and I began incorporating images from the plumbing catalogs.

I studied art history at the Institute of Fine Arts at N.Y.U. and did an M.A. thesis on Picabia and Duchamp. It was one of the roughest things I ever did, and I don't know why I did it. But in a roundabout way it was how I met a lot of people. I published an article from the thesis on Picabia (he died while I was writing it) in *Arts* magazine, which came out just about the same time I had my first one-man show (sometime in 1955). I met Tom Hess (editor of *Art News*) that way. He didn't like the rough draft of the article I wrote, said it was too serious. So I gave it to Hilton Kramer (editor of *Arts*), and he turned it over to an editor, who rewrote it. I got to know Kramer by insisting on being allowed to rewrite it myself. I wanted it my own way. I wrote about ten articles on different things that Hess published over the years. All together I have published about sixteen or seventeen articles, and each one has meant a lot of work. Time away from painting. But I did write one called "Figure Paintings Today Are Not Made in Heaven" that changed the course of my own development.

It was '61. The Museum of Modern Art was having a big figure-painting show, after the "New Images of Man" show, and Hess wanted to know if I was interested in writing about it. I went to see the work that they had collected and found there was no straightforward representational painting in it. So I sat down to write the introduction to the criticism of the show and the introduction just kept growing and I spoke to Hess about what I should do. He said, "Just keep writing. Let it grow." I systematically analyzed the various approaches that could be taken or were taken to represent the figure. I didn't know it then, but what I had done was outline the way my own work was going to develop. What I also got out of doing the piece was a kind of schizoid attitude toward painting. I realized that there's a real gap between intellect and doing, and that if you wanted to really paint, do anything with your finger skills, you have to stop thinking. You cannot think and paint at the same time. So in between bouts of writing these articles I don't think.

Although I felt I knew all there was to know about modernism and I was free to do what I wanted to do, my work began evolving again under the impact of abstract expressionism. It became very brushy, very thick and more monochromatic, with less blatant separate areas of color. I got involved in painting rocks, just rock forms. On a trip across the country I stopped at the Petrified Forest, the Grand Canyon, and a couple of other places out west, and I picked up rocks, pieces of petrified wood, and they became my models. Later, on Montauk Point at the end of Long Island, I picked up a whole bushel-basketful of rocks, took them back to the studio, and made watercolors and drawings from them. Then I made oil paintings from the watercolors and drawings. The final oil paintings looked pretty abstract—a combination of painting styles from de Kooning, Franz Kline, back to Cézanne and Gauguin. It was very difficult to find a subject matter in them. They were the kind of paintings that I had in my first one-man show at the Tanager Gallery. Eventually, in the summer of 1956, up in Maine, I made a series of brush drawings of rock formations that were quite accurate. And then later, after I got back to New York, I did very expressionist paintings from those rocks. Views of boulders and rocks piled up along the edge of the water.

When I went to Rome on a Fulbright Fellowship I did the same thing, very straightforward brush drawings, elaborately worked out—with the Roman ruins. I left the Peridot Gallery because they didn't want to show the Roman drawings. They put prices like $35 or $50 on them, but I'd been doing commercial work and knew that the amount of time I put into those drawings compared to whatever I was getting as a commercial artist didn't make sense. So I added zeros to the prices when the drawings were shown at the Tanager.

SEATED NUDE LEANING ON CHAIR
1966. Pencil, 20 × 26 in. Private collection.

PHILIP PEARLSTEIN

NUDE ON MEXICAN BLANKET
1972. Oil on canvas, 40 × 48 in.
Collection of Fine Arts Center, Colorado Springs.

CROUCHING NUDE WITH MIRROR
1971. Oil on canvas, 60 × 48 in.
Collection of the artist.

Instead of being about $35 or $40, they were $350 or $400. Dore Ashton gave them a big review, and about six of them sold at what were then high prices. Then Allan Frumkin took me on, and the first show I had there were paintings based on those drawings (1961). But the paintings, looking at them now, were more like Philip Guston than anybody else. Guston in the early fifties. They were kind of patchy, misty. But they were already beginning to get more realistic. They were big scale for the time—six-by-eight feet, some of them. When I finished all those paintings, I had the feeling that the drawings represented something else that was maybe truer to me. The drawings were more architectonic, not expressionistic, no flurries of brush mark or any of that.

At about that time I had joined a drawing group and began dealing with figures. I was doing figure drawings the same way I did the Roman landscapes. I was looking for abstract structure in nature. Cutting off my figures at the picture edge actually came from working with rocks; my figures were an extension of them. The rocks, the peaks, the ruins were huge, so they moved off the page. One just led into the other. And, of course, that was a tremendous help in my getting rid of expressionist mannerisms. The drawing became very coordinated, the figures in space became convincing. I didn't worry about what they meant, I wasn't concerned about subject matter as such; they were just models in the studio. I felt I had put aside all symbolistic references. And that became my kind of realism.

I began teaching about that same time. I think teaching is actually what changed my whole idea about painting, getting rid of the expressionist, as much of the arbitrary abstraction as I could.

In 1972 I won an award from the American Academy of Arts and Letters, so I went with my wife and three kids to Massa Lubrense, which we'd seen the year before. It was very pretty and I thought it was a nice place to spend the summer. I made two paintings there. Four-foot-square paintings. One was a cliff and another was a view along the coast. Those were in the show I had that year at Frumkin's. Then they were in a big Chicago art show. And I guess John Arthur, who organized the Department of the Interior show for the 1976 Bicentennial celebration, saw them there. And that led me to the Canyon de Chelly in Arizona to do a painting for him. This last trip back to Rome in 1982 (I was an Artist in Residence at the American Academy), I did a view of old Rome from the roof of the Villa Aurelea, a spectacular sixteenth-century building, one of the Farnese Palaces, and Garibaldi's headquarters during his first campaign. Apparently the French were on the other side of the Aurelian Wall, which is right there. And they were shelling and he was shelling. I can just picture him up on that roof looking out over Rome. I had a great time up there. I spent seven days doing this piece. I picked the angle because the Roman ruins run right through the center of the picture. Everything that I spent painting that winter of 1958–59 is there in that view in miniature. It's a watercolor, forty inches wide.

The thing I've always gone after almost immediately, from the very start, working with rocks and then working with the real landscape and then painting from the figures in the studio, is trying to find a compositional structure in the subject itself, in nature. It's a kind of structure that is not so different from the structure I read in the paintings of, say, de Kooning and Kline; just the way the forms move across the surface. I simply saw the rocks, the way two rocks meet each other, move away, or the way Roman ruins meet the ground, or the way a tree meets the ground. You get long movements if you think of the axis of the forms. It's just the clash of the axes that the picture structure is based on—diagonal, opposing movements. And I translate that directly into the movement of the figure, how the models are posed, how they move against the pieces of furniture. I rely on the angle where the wall meets the floor as a constant reference point, and against that I oppose the movements of the models' limbs. With the addition of furniture, draperies like Japanese kimonos or rugs, other movements are created, and the relationship between forms is much more complex. That's actually what the paintings are about.

The color comes from observation. I try not to add any color that I can't see. In the first years, the color of the figure paintings was pretty drab-looking. The floor that I was working against was gray. Then I tried other colors. There was a series of paintings where the plywood floor was painted tan. Then I hit on a green floor that I saw in somebody's loft, and I've been using that ever since, because it works against the body color of the model so well. But the color I use is really an attempt to be as accurate in color as I am in drawing the contours of the forms. Using rugs, pieces of furniture, gives me a chance to bring in a greater range of color than just using the models.

I hate to say it, but a lot of the things I did in the army—at least in relation to drawing and color—are really quite close to what I've been doing the last few years with figures and landscapes. In between came the excursions into expressionism and symbolism.

WHITE HOUSE RUIN, CANYON DE CHELLY: AFTERNOON
1975. Oil on canvas, 60 × 60 in.
Courtesy Allan Frumkin Gallery, New York.

CLIFF AT MASSA LUBRENSE
1973. Oil on canvas, 48 × 48 in.
Collection of Dr. and Mrs. Milton Shiffman.

FEMALE MODEL ON CAST IRON BED
1975. Oil on canvas, 48 × 60 in.
The Art Museum, Princeton University.

FEMALE MODEL ON BROCADE SOFA
1975. Oil on canvas, 60 × 48 in.
Collection of Steven D. Robinson.

PHILIP PEARLSTEIN

99

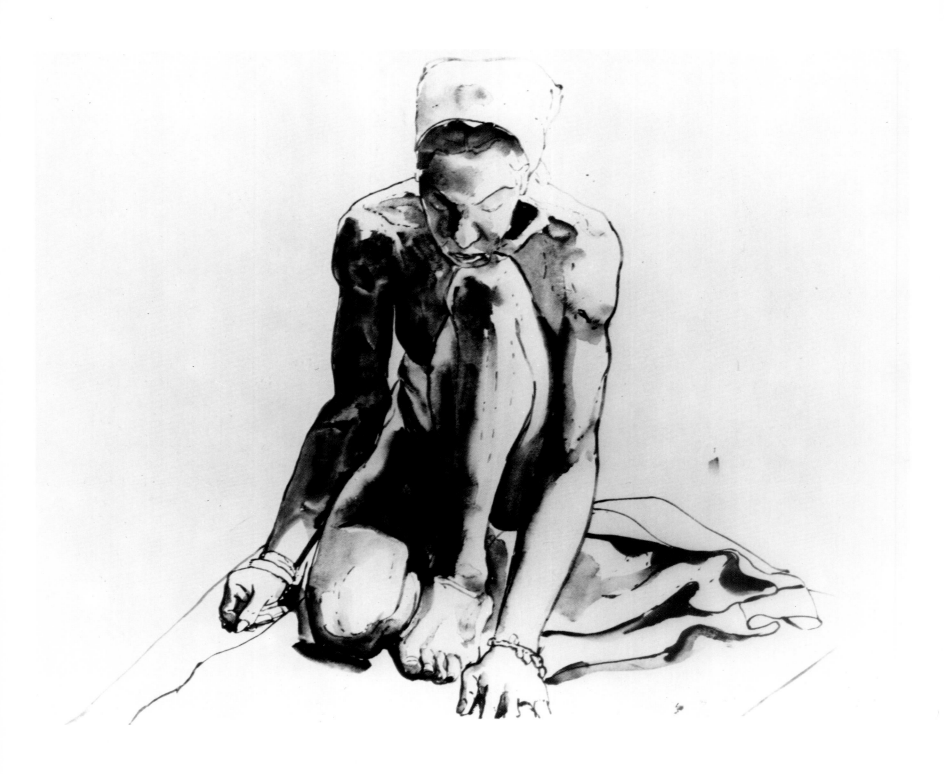

KNEELING FIGURE (STUDY FOR CROUCHING NUDE WITH BANDANNA)
1967. Sepia on paper, 22 × 30 in.
Collection of the artist.

PHILIP PEARLSTEIN

Gradually I've worked my way back. In terms of subject matter, not much has changed over the years. I recently found a little oil painting from my high-school days of the people in a streetcar; it doesn't show a real concern for the people so much as an attempt to look at them objectively. Putting them in a social context made it look as though I had more sympathy for them than just curiosity.

I've deliberately tried not to be expressive about the models I've been painting for almost twenty years now, not to make any kind of comment but just to work at the formal problems of representational painting in relation to picture structure. But even though I try to remain objective, it looks as though I'm concerned about the people. I know that the paintings disturb a lot of people who insist on reading something into them. I guess if I looked at them as an outsider, I would begin to see disturbing things in them, too. But I'm not really concerned with that and I don't want to be concerned with that. It's an aspect of painting that can't be controlled. No artist can really control what people read in the work. So maybe it *looks* like the paintings are saying something about the human condition, but I don't feel I control that. I remember reading something Raphael Soyer said in an interview when somebody commented on the fact that his figures always looked unhappy; he said he didn't know how it happened, it just happened. When he painted me in a painting, I saw him transform me into one of his very soulful-looking people, although neither he nor I were feeling especially soulful.

I think the same thing happens with every artist, every authentic artist. A look is produced by the way the work is developed, and meanings somehow are on a very subjective, unconscious level. You run into trouble when you try to put it into words, especially if you're the artist and you try to define what it is that you want to express. I've heard a number of people, figurative people, speak about their aims, and I've almost never been able to see in the work itself what they thought the work meant.

I've painted a lot of portraits, some of my children, some of my friends, and some were commissioned. Generally, with the commissioned portraits I don't know the person before I start painting. I get to know them during the course of it. But I never try to express anything about them, I just try to bring the same kind of objectivity that I feel I bring to the paintings of the models. I try to establish some compositional scheme that would be interesting and start from there. I let the people find their own positions and make their own gestures. I don't guide them or give them directions. I don't want to choose the clothes. I prefer that they wear what they want to wear. I do believe there is a body language that says something about people, but I'd rather those gestures came from the people themselves, and I just paint them as carefully as I can, the features of the face, the expressions of the face while they are sitting there. And it's not meant to be a universal picture of them for all time. If they look bored or tired during those working sessions, unfortunately that's what comes through. I've tried to get away from the boredom look by having them look at a small TV. I set it up right next to myself so that at least they're looking in my direction with some kind of interest, and not staring blankly into space. But that's as far as I'll go in terms of controlling what the final painting will show of the people.

When I work with the models, I play records all the time. It's the kind of situation that gives them something to focus on without getting in the way and it keeps the level of conversation down. When the record ends, which is usually in twenty-five to thirty minutes, the model takes a break. Then we talk for five or ten minutes. I do know the models as people, but I'm not concerned with saying anything about them in the paintings other than that they are reasonably intelligent. I think that comes through body gesture, and not through playing around with facial expressions. It's never become easier, I've never figured out formulas. It may look as if I have. The only routine is that the models are there, the same paints are there. It's a deliberately limited and artificial situation.

TEMPLES AT ABOU SIMBEL
1979. Watercolor, 29 × 41 in.
Collection of the artist.

THE GREAT SPHINX
1979. Watercolor, 29¼ × 41½ in.
The Toledo Museum of Art, Toledo, Ohio.
© Toledo Museum of Art, 1979.

PHILIP PEARLSTEIN

RECLINING FEMALE MODEL
1969. Wash on paper, 22 × 30 in.
Private collection.

PHILIP PEARLSTEIN

I've been going back to landscape a lot, but not with oil paint. I find it much easier to use watercolor in a landscape situation to keep up with changing light. I can be more accurate with watercolor from the beginning. But even there I seem to limit the situation in a way. I've limited the landscape to ruins. I won't do the landscape unless there's a ruin out there. I've wondered about that as a subject matter, and why I keep coming back to ruins. I think that in some way it's tied up with my exposure to the Roman ruins during the years I spent in Italy during the war. And probably there's something emotional or poetic on a subconscious level operating there that I admit to, much more than there is with my use of models. When I work with a model it's always a kind of reference to the sort of experience I had with art back in my highschool years. The landscapes came from my war years, simply because my first contact with landscape, looking at landscape, thinking about landscape, came during the time I was in the army. Being in the infantry, I came to see a lot of landscape at a very close hand. And whenever I paint the ruins, or set up on a site, I get a big kick out of turning that place into my studio for a couple of days. When I was working at Stonehenge, a tourist walked by and told his wife I wanted to take Stonehenge home with me. And I guess that sums it up. My watercolors are like models, miniature models, of the area of the ruin, and I want to take it home.

I owe a great deal to the painters of the 1950s in New York City. They were my true education in painting. Even though I didn't really know them on a personal level, I learned through looking at their work and analyzing it in my own terms. My involvement with realism, when I did work my way back to it, was based on adapting their ideas to my ways of seeing the world, and into my ideas about making paintings.

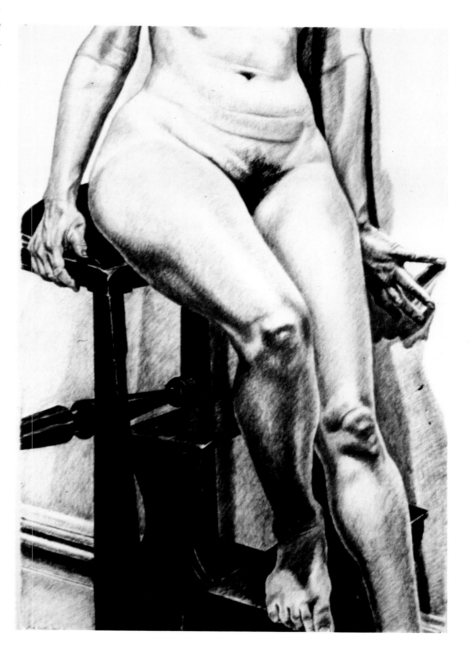

MODEL ON LIBRARY LADDER
1982. Charcoal, 44¼ × 30¼ in.
Courtesy Allan Frumkin Gallery, New York.

TWO MODELS IN BAMBOO CHAIRS
1981. Oil on canvas, 60 × 72 in.
Collection of Rosanne Diamond Zinn.

PHILIP PEARLSTEIN

TWO MODELS IN BAMBOO CHAIRS WITH MIRROR
1981. Oil on canvas, $72\frac{3}{16} \times 72\frac{1}{8}$ in.
The Toledo Museum of Art, Toledo, Ohio. © Toledo Museum of Art, 1981.

PHILIP PEARLSTEIN

Of course we are all educated in the art of Europe and the ancient classical world; I have even taught survey courses in art history. But the 1950s art world of New York—I mean the group of artists known as action painters or abstract expressionists—was a mythic, heroic world. At least it seemed so to me then and still does. Though I was not part of that central group I was active on the fringe, faithfully attended the discussions at the Club, and caught up in the sense of painting as an exploration, an exhilarating adventure. It's easy to sentimentalize about the 1950s now, but I still thrill when I see the best works of that time. I believe that sense of creativity as a way of life, where every new developing canvas was a matter of utmost urgency, has remained with me. It seemed to me then that what mattered most to that group was how paint reacted to manipulation by brushes, rags, hands, the artist's gestures. Color was secondary, drawing was almost unthought of. But by degrees color and drawing became more important to individual artists until by 1960 emphasis on those attributes split the art world apart. Gesture was superseded by careful control and color dictated form for many of the younger, as well as older, artists. The importance of drawing in my work had surged and demanded equality with color and careful paint handling. I finally realized its basis in my work and that set me off on my ongoing painted exploration of the human figure.

TWO MODELS SEATED ON MEXICAN BLANKET
1982. Charcoal, 30 × 44 in.
Courtesy Allan Frumkin Gallery, New York.

TWO MODELS ON KILIM RUG WITH MIRROR
1982. Charcoal on canvas, 90 × 72 in.
(Painted over)

PHILIP PEARLSTEIN

PAESTUM
1982. Watercolor on paper, 29½ × 41 in.
Collection of the artist.

VIEW OF ROME
1982. Watercolor on paper, 29½ × 41 in.
Courtesy Allan Frumkin Gallery, New York.

Alex Katz

I knew I'd be some kind of artist. I didn't think I'd be a fine artist. I thought I'd be a commercial artist. My parents had friends who were painters in Russia, so we had paintings on the walls when I was growing up, and I used to draw with my father. There were books around the house, too. As I grew up I found that my parent's culture was different from mine. They were from Europe. I wasn't into their culture and they weren't into mine. There were no problems being a painter or an intellectual, coming from my family. I didn't have any of the problems with parents that most artists have with their parents. My family wasn't negative, they weren't neutral, they actually encouraged me.

As a kid I felt I was never really terrific at "art." There was a guy in the neighborhood who could draw much better than I could. And he ended up being an extremely successful commercial artist. When he was nineteen he was making more money than any father on the block. When he was twenty-one he was even richer. He was one of these guys that was made for advertising. He wanted to take me with him. He said, "Al, you come along with me." But I was going to Cooper Union and it was too much fun. This was right

after World War II. And I went to Cooper to study commercial art. I was kidding myself, because I was taking more and more fine art courses. He said, "Why waste your time in school? Come with me and make a bundle and blow it all away." He had none of the vanity of a person with a lesser ambition. He had no vanity. He had real ambition, and he was ruthless. He was after his boss's job when he was twenty-two. It was a real big job. He was out of art work by the time he was in his mid-twenties and was into real executive stuff. Then he died in an automobile accident.

It was thirteen years before I got a place with a radiator in it. I worked in frame shops for ten years. And I think it was fifteen years before I did sell my paintings to pay the rent. That's the rougher end of it as far as that goes. And I think when you're young you like that sort of thing, you're struggling along. And I liked it a little more than most people. I had no help from my family. By then my father was dead and my mother had to help herself. In fact, I felt a little bit like I should help her out. And my brother wasn't doing anything either, so it was like the whole family was on the skids.

My first two shows were at the Roko Gallery. It was

THE RED SMILE
1963. Oil on canvas, $78\frac{3}{4} \times 114\frac{3}{4}$ in.
Collection of Whitney Museum of American Art.

ADA FOUR TIMES
1968. Oil on metal cut-out, $58\frac{1}{4} \times 43\frac{1}{2}$ in.
Collection of Dr. and Mrs. Terry Podolsky.

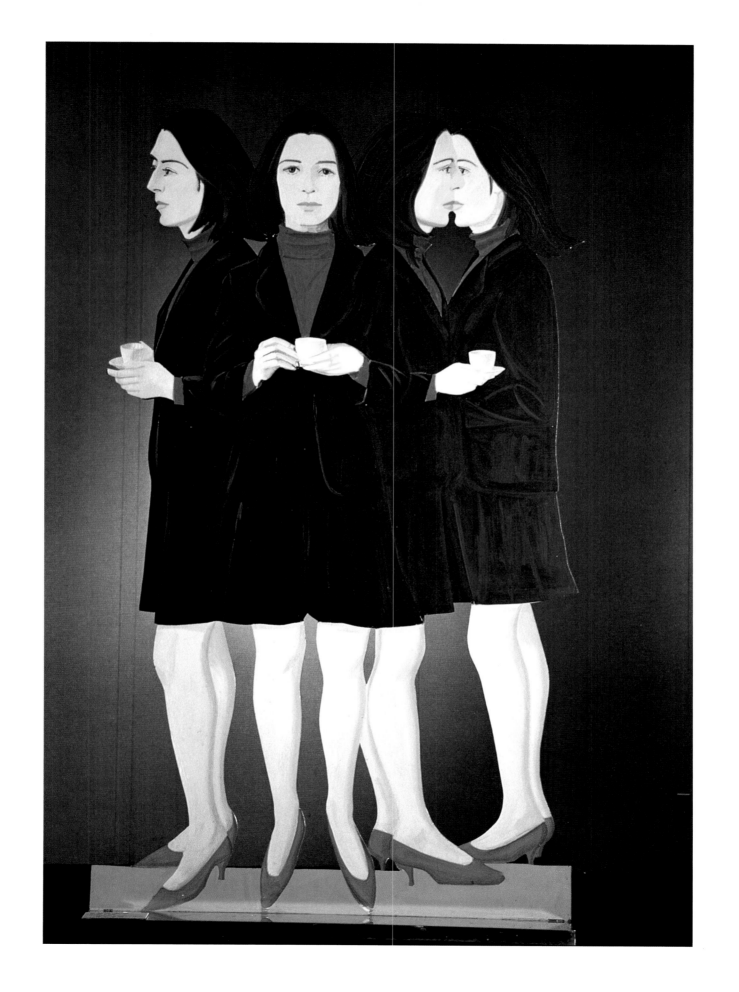

like a frame shop. And I sold one little thing to a guy I was working for. He was a muralist by the name of Maragliotti and we were doing work that he was going to get paid for. He couldn't do the work. He had gotten the job with his ex-partner's samples. It was *trompe l'oeil* painting. In other words, we thought we had him over a barrel. He was such a nice guy, what with spaghetti dinners and whiskey, he kept us smil-ing. One of the things he did when I had a show was to race down and buy a painting. So, in essence, he bought my ass for seventy-five bucks. And he knew it and I knew it, but the guy had such charm, he just said, "You learn something about life this way." Anyhow, that was the first show at Roko, and the second was when Roko moved up to Madison Avenue, and that was run about the same way.

ALEX KATZ

ROGER
1977. Pencil on paper, 15 × 22 in.
Courtesy Marlborough Gallery, New York.

THOMAS
1975. Pencil, 15 × 21¾ in.
Courtesy Marlborough Gallery, New York.

FACE OF A POET
1972. Oil on canvas, 114 × 210 in.
Collection of Paul Jacques Schupf.

EVENING
1972. Oil on canvas, 72 × 96 in.
Collection of Mr. and Mrs. John A. Lawrence.
Courtesy Marlborough Gallery, New York.

Then I went down to the Tanager Gallery on Tenth Street and I had a show there. The artists were the people who started to buy my work.

I think I was on my fifth show when I started to support myself with painting. I sold a cutout to Elaine de Kooning for three hundred bucks. I think it was, oh, my seventh, eighth, ninth show, about half my sales were to artists. So I found a public, an art public, way before I found a commercial public or an institutional one and it was very encouraging. Anyhow, that's the way it was. I spent the fifties on the street, so to speak; it was very public. People were out on the streets and talking and everything. It wasn't too bad.

In the late fifties I started reading poetry and I found I liked Kenneth Koch and Frank O'Hara's poetry and then Jimmy Schuyler's. Actually, I used to read poetry

LAURA DEAN DANCE COMPANY
1977. Ink on paper, $8\frac{1}{4} \times 10\frac{5}{8}$ in.
Courtesy Marlborough Gallery, New York.

ROSE ROOM II
1981. Ink on paper, 8½ × 11 in.
Courtesy Marlborough Gallery, New York.

a lot when I was in the navy. There was some guy who used to read it. He was a hoody type. A real bad man, but he read poetry. Anyhow, we started to read poetry, and I had trouble with it but I liked reading it. I've always liked poetry because I've never understood it. When I started to read the New York things I could understand them, and through them I was able to read older things and get much more out of them, really understand them. I guess it was in '55 or '56 that

I met Edwin Denby, also Rudy Burckhardt. Edwin was a poet and he knew all the poets and it seemed exciting to me. Actually, in the sixties a whole crowd came in from Tulsa and really made the New York school, Padgett and Berrigan, Gallup and Brainard. They gave the New York school a kind of focus. Their energy was connected. And I felt connected to them, whereas the older artists were reading Sartre and Camus. I really couldn't take that stuff very seriously.

I could read it, and sort of understand it, but almost every young painter, every second-generation painter would have a Camus book on the coffee table. I was much more interested in dancing and basketball, in having a good time. Those artists who were reading Camus . . . I felt I couldn't live the kind of life I was living or like the kind of things I liked and take that sort of thing seriously. The young poets seemed much closer to where I was. I had no intellectual position; for me it was all instinctive. I think people like Denby operated out of an aesthetic that made sense. So I sort of picked that up, mostly from Edwin, in the middle or late fifties. It was part of my on-the-street education. But I'm not as heavily involved in the poetry as I was ten years ago. I like seeing young artists' shows more. I like to see lively stuff.

I like my painting to deal mostly with appearance. Style and appearance are the things that I'm more concerned about than what something means. I'd like to have style take the place of content, or the style be the

STUDY FOR ADA AND FLOWERS
1980. Pencil on paper, 14¾ × 22 in.
Collection of the American Academy and
Institute of Arts and Letters, New York.

MEREDITH
1980. Pencil on paper, 15 × 22 in.
Courtesy Marlborough Gallery, New York.

ALEX KATZ

ANNE AND BILLY
1981. Graphite on paper, 15½ × 22½ in.
Collection of Paul Jacques Schupf.

content. It doesn't have to be beefed up by meaning. In fact, I prefer it to be emptied of meaning, emptied of content.

To me there's an enormous difference between something that's stylized and something that has style. Stylized is like a cheap way to make handwriting identifiable. Whereas style is a much broader thing. It covers more ground. When something's stylized it doesn't cover much ground, all it does is give you the identity of the author in a quick way.

I think of style as being a conscious choice. Everything you do in your life ends up the next day with your making a choice. It's one thing built right on the next. One's behavior is determined by one's previous behaviors. I think that has to do with style.

For new compositions I make little sketches. I can't spend a lot of time on one of those sketch paintings. I generally paint the sketches very quickly. And it has to do with an idea of quick light. My paintings must have an instantaneous quality. Anyway, my paintings start with those little sketches, which are instantaneous impressions. Afterward, I'll make drawings. They are done very slowly because when you make something instantaneous things get a little generalized. When I make a drawing, I take the time to move a line this way, move a line that way, make a shadow darker, change my proportions, move the gesture around a little bit. All this enables me to paint the final painting quickly. What other painters might do on one surface, I do on many. The sketches and drawings are stages I go through on the way to that final painting. My painting is like a performance. And those things are almost like rehearsals. I want a consistent surface, a consistent, smooth surface, and I want to have a fairly complicated figuration, and the only way I can do that is to preplan a great deal of it.

I want large paintings with a lot of muscle, so I work out the figuration in the size I want. Last summer I spent the whole summer on a painting of three cows in a field. And the smallest I could make the painting

ADA IN COAT
1982. Graphite on paper, $22\frac{1}{2} \times 15\frac{1}{2}$ in.
Collection of Paul Jacques Schupf.

was eight feet by twelve. It wouldn't make any sense to paint that picture smaller. It wouldn't have had any effect smaller. It just would be a dull painting. And once I did a canoe and I had to make the damn thing twelve feet so it would appear the way a canoe would appear. So that the scale of my paintings is not only determined by what I unconsciously feel about the rightness of the space, but somehow whatever is painted has to assume some of the scale it has in life. Painting can become something that's one-on-one with what you're seeing, but sometimes it's different. For instance, you can go up to a Watteau and see little figures on the canvas and all of a sudden they seem the right size. You accept them as life size.

There are two ways for twentieth-century painters to work. One way is to build as you go along. You put a figure here, then you take it out and you move it over, and you add a figure—that's like Picasso, it's short of a construction method. The other method is like Barnett Newman. You just put the figure in the middle of the canvas, that's arrangement. I do something that's more complicated and it's with compositions where there are a lot of moving parts. And to work with moving parts you have to preplan. It's impossible to arrive at convincing gestures of people in a fluid style without preplanning. That's the way it is. My paintings are preplanned in a way. But you can't preplan everything—you leave enough room for it to be opened up in painting. Even as you're working on the sketches you're thinking of the size of the canvas.

I like being restricted, held down in motifs. I've tried painting the same thing over and over for the past twenty years. When I was a kid I used to ride my bike twenty miles, looking for things to paint. Then my father asked, "Why don't you paint your own backyard?" My father was right. So I stick pretty close to home. All those paintings up in Maine. All those paintings of Ada. Part of what I'm about is seeing how I can paint the same thing differently instead of different things the same way.

Among realist paintings I think my paintings are more modern than most. When I was asked to describe what I was trying to do twenty years ago I said, "Brand new and terrific." I like my paintings to look brand new. I think of myself as a modern person and I want my painting to look that way. I think of my paintings as different from some others in that they derive a lot from modern paintings as well as from older paintings. I would say that makes them distinctive. They're traditional because all painting belongs to the paintings before them, and they're modernistic because they're responsive to the immediate. When my son went to the island of Crete he said, "These paintings"—he was looking at the murals there— "these have a lot to do with your paintings. You may think Rembrandt has more to do with your paintings, but these do." He was right. And I find that I've gotten a lot out of Egyptian work. I've certainly gotten a lot out of the Japanese. And I think Watteau is just like the end. I've looked at all kinds of different things and I find that they seem to relate to each other. In a blink you can go from an Egyptian painting to a Matisse and then on to something modern.

My prime value I think is generally light and gesture. So I have less detail than most realist painters, but my light is more specific than most realists, it's a more realistic light. It's specific and actual. And my surfaces are more realistic than most because of the light and the color. The light is conceived through color, and because of that I get more convincing surfaces: Air, water, trees, they're all optically realistic. For me it's mostly image and appearance. I'm interested in taking people from the world I live in. Sometimes it's old tales with new clothes, sometimes it's just new clothes. But always I want my images to be lively. I want a sense of liveliness for the imagery.

BICYCLE RIDER
1982. Oil on canvas, 72 × 96 in.
Courtesy Marlborough Gallery, New York.

TRACY ON THE RAFT AT 7:30
1982. Oil on canvas, 120 × 72 in.
Courtesy Marlborough Gallery, New York.

Lennart Anderson

My father held on to his job at Ford in Detroit during the Depression. He was a pattern maker and Ford was developing the V-8. When we moved into a large brick house around 1931, there was an alcoholic saw-filer and his wife living in one of the apartments. I discovered him drawing one day—a picture of a worker chained to his bench—a drawing I remember to this day. I also recall my mother, to amuse my brother and me, copying Johnny Walker in pencil from a newspaper ad. She has always encouraged me. When my older brother brought his drawings back from kindergarten—strange little people with big foreheads walking in houses with the sides off so you could see inside—I copied those too. I betrayed no ability or imagination, just desire. In school, my first art teacher looked at me in wonder when I showed her drawings of collie dogs and windjammers. I begged to be let into the special art class after school, to no avail. My next teacher was pleased to find someone so interested in drawing. She let me into the class. By this time I was spending Sundays at the art museum. It was there that I learned about Pearl Harbor.

I had been pleading for oil paints for a long time. My father thought only professionals should have them, but when Lewis Art Supply had a fire sale in 1942 I was given a beautiful little wood case with Orpen colors for Christmas. I began to go to the School of Arts & Crafts in 1943 near downtown Detroit on Saturday afternoons, painting from the model. The class was made up mostly of people who were graduates of the school and who wanted to paint from the figure. The atmosphere was very serious, and the teachers, Sarkis Sarkisian and Guy Palazzola, who, with great patience, would bring my broken tones back together, were excellent. The perfect place for a fervent young soul.

I attended Cass Technical High School in Detroit. A curriculum called Commercial Art had been set up to prepare artists for the auto industry. It was a fine school, but I think we suffered some in not getting a rounded education. With the experience Cass provided, scholarships to art school were not difficult to obtain. Mine was to the School of the Art Institute in Chicago for September 1946.

The Art Institute was filled with returning GIs. In fact, my class had only two others from high school. I had some trouble with the design course. I couldn't compose with abstract shapes and then put subject matter into them. Nonetheless, I learned a lot from this course—things about pattern, shape, and variety.

ACCIDENT (STREET SCENE)
1955–1957. Oil on canvas, 47 × 57 in.
Collection of Museum of Art,
The Pennsylvania State University.

LENNART ANDERSON

138

STREET SCENE
1961. Oil on canvas, 79 × 99 in.
Collection of the artist.

LENNART ANDERSON

Almost all of our time was devoted to painting and drawing from the model. But I am afraid we did it in a spirit of marking time. None of us expected to be painting that way when we left school. There was no enthusiastic teaching of the figure that made it relevant or exciting. The atmosphere wasn't right for it. I doubt that we would have accepted it in any case.

There were mainly three teachers of painting at the Art Institute in those years. Boris Anisfeld, a painter and stage designer from Russia who was quite famous in the twenties; Louis Ritman, a painter who spent years in Paris before the war and who knew Soutine; and Paul Wieghardt, from Germany, who taught a kind of Paul Klee–Edouard Jacques Villon sensitivity to color relationships. I ruled out Wieghardt immediately as being too precious, and first enrolled in Anisfeld's class. He was a stocky, powerful man with bangs and a beard. The work done in his class had color pushed to extremes—very hot, very cold, with a creamy look to the whites. He professed a love for Velázquez, however, and I, taking him at his word, painted very tonally. My work began to attract attention from freshmen who would wander into class during the long break. I was embarrassed and would leave the room. Anisfeld became very angry and finally launched into an attack on all my work in front of the class. His complaint was I was not using color. But looking around me, I was not about to use Anisfeld color, so at the end of one semester I left.

I gravitated to Ritman. His class was very relaxed. No one ever found out what Ritman had to teach. I was attracted to the class by Maury Lapp, a student whom I admired, who seemed to set a serious tenor. His sketchbooks were filled with pure expressionism, and I ached to paint like Kokoschka, Soutine, and Roualt. This was the time of the gestation of the Chicago Monster school; Leon Golub, Ted Halkin, and Cosmo Compoli were all students at the time. During the last semester, I decided to apply to Cranbrook Academy of Art for an advanced degree.

Cranbrook in 1950 gave a master's degree without requiring any classroom work. Each student was given a place in which to paint or sculpt and was expected to more or less work out his own problems. I was told, however, that considering my previous experience I should not work from life. This was no hardship, because I planned to paint expressionistically. I painted a picture of two dried-up red peppers thirty by forty-two inches, another of a dead baby, another of a female corpse, one of a street scene with men warming their hands over a fire in a trash barrel. I loved painting these pictures. But before the year was out I realized that expressionism was, for me, a formal approach and one that I was tiring of. With a couple months of school yet to go, I decided to do portraits of the students. I asked $15 apiece so I could be sure of having models. The teacher had the grace to ignore what was going on, since I seemed bent on ignoring his advice about painting from the model. I concentrated on the head, painting them usually in one sitting with likeness a major consideration. When the semester ended I had saved $130, enough for my first trip to New York.

When I was in New York I visited a fellow student, whose father had the auction catalogs of Degas's studio contents: Hundreds of drawings, pastels, and paintings were reproduced. I was very excited by this austere man, whose work reflected such pain, almost disgust, as well as passion for his goal. His heroic effort to maintain the nude as a noble subject for art, inspired me, and still does.

Going back to school in September 1951, I wanted to do a street scene with a figure in the air. Painters once had access to subjects that allowed this routinely. Tintoretto's *Miracle of St. Mark* was a picture that excited me. I wanted in a similar way to get a figure off the ground, unattached and moving. Working on this idea, Zoltan Sepeshy, my instructor, mentioned a famous photograph of a drop of milk splashing into a dish at impact with a symmetrical crown of drops thrown up. I decided to try the painting from that view. I wanted to paint an emotional subject (Manet, after all, had painted a suicide) without an expressionist approach, to paint as if I were only an observer.

STREET SCENE
1959. Oil on panel, 16¼ × 20½ in.
Collection of Robert C. Graham, Jr.

LENNART ANDERSON

141

STILL LIFE WITH BLACK CUP
1953. Oil on canvas, 14 × 18 in.
From the collection of Mr. and Mrs. Paul Mellon,
Upperville, Virginia.

NUDE ON CHAIR
1965. Oil on canvas, 60 × 50 in.
Courtesy Davis & Langdale Company, Inc.

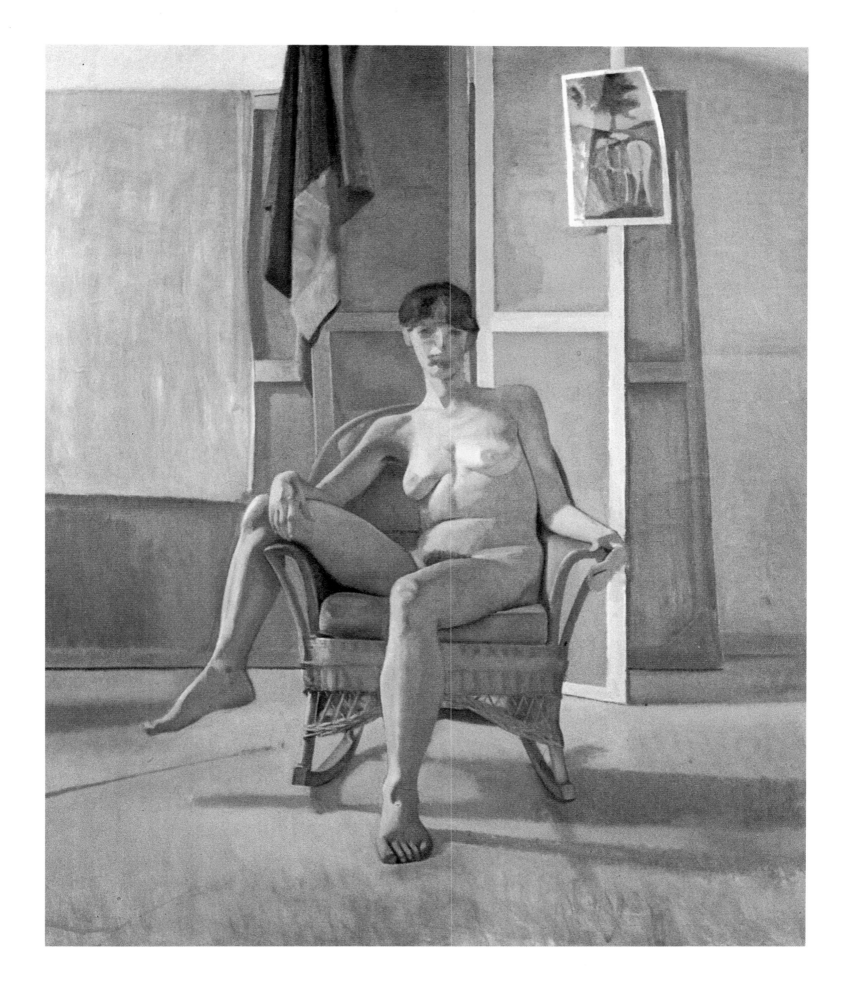

I painted part of the word "Stop" in a sign in the distance and included a clergyman turning and running away in the foreground. In the painting the figure in the air could be compared to paper blowing in the street. Though the subject may be depressing, it was not my intention to paint a scene of horror but instead to show the grace of the moment. It was an Italian, not a Flemish, martyrdom that I was trying to paint.

After finishing school, I returned to Detroit, renting a tiny servant's room on the top floor of an apartment house overlooking the Detroit River. In order to make room to paint I had to turn my cot on its side. In such a space I devoted myself to small still lifes. But I began to feel that I could not stay in Detroit. I could not afford to be a failure there. My father, who had worked so hard, was looking on. My painting was too old-fashioned for the town. Also, I knew no other painters to talk to. New York seemed some sort of a solution. I had been reading Fairfield Porter's reviews in *Art News* and felt they must represent more than a single person's viewpoint. I needed to feel part of a society that supported me emotionally. Even if I didn't particularly take part in it, I wanted to feel that it was there. So in August 1953 I left for New York.

I came to New York with two weavers, Jeanne McIntyre and Ruben Eshkanian, and another painter, Richard Serrin. Jeanne and Ruben opened a weaving and textile shop on Sheridan Square. Richard and I shared a garret on Thirty-eighth Street around the corner from Lord & Taylor, where we both got jobs, which were to last through the Christmas shopping season. We both hated the work and quit on the same day in October without conferring with each other. We decided to go back home, but to prevent the whole adventure from being a total loss I decided to try and find a gallery to handle my work. Fairfield Porter had written some reviews for the Davis Gallery on Sixtieth Street, and I thought I should try it; their painters seemed as dull as I was. Mr. Davis was surprised to see work like mine, especially since it came from the Midwest. When he said he couldn't take me solely on what he could see, I told him my plan to go back to Detroit. He said that he thought I should stay in New York. He asked me whether I would stay if he could find a job for me. I said sure. So he picked up the phone and dialed one digit. After a short conversation, he told me to report the next morning to Robert Kulicke's, where I would be put to work cutting and joining frames. I said I had absolutely no ability to do that kind of work, but he said not to worry and to just show up. So I started working two and a half days a week and found a room on East Seventy-fourth Street, three blocks from the shop. I took a class with Edwin Dickinson for two months, not long enough to absorb his teaching. I passionately admired his work.

One of the students at Cranbrook who had been kind and supportive to my work was Pat Pasloff. A New Yorker, who had studied with de Kooning at Black Mountain, she had a loft on the famous block on Tenth Street that housed so many abstract expressionists. She held a kind of open house, it was either that or everyone took advantage of her hospitality. There I met the painters Milton Resnick, Esteban Vicente, Aristidemos Kaldis, Landis Lewiten, and an assortment of people that also included writers, dancers, even mathematicians. I was accepted there as a painter, but no one other than Pat and Milton knew what kind of painting I did. Pat wanted me to get more into the swing of things and persuaded Milton to put me up for the Club, a loft on Broadway where on Friday night artists met to hash over whatever seemed to be going on at the time. I remember a long series of panel discussions devoted to "nature," a curious subject for an organization dominated by abstract artists. There was an excitement about these meetings. Reputations seemed to be forming there. I felt attracted and intimidated at the same time. I sometimes wondered whether the idea was to speak for twenty minutes without giving oneself away.

In the summer of 1954 Pat Pasloff found a small loft across the street from hers on Tenth Street, and I moved in. I began painting a street scene in a style

PORTRAIT OF BARBARA S.
1976. Oil on canvas, 97 × 72 in.
Courtesy of the Pennsylvania Academy
of the Fine Arts.

ST. MARK'S PLACE
1969–75. Oil on canvas, 97 × 72 in.
Collection of University of Virginia Art Museum,
Charlottesville.

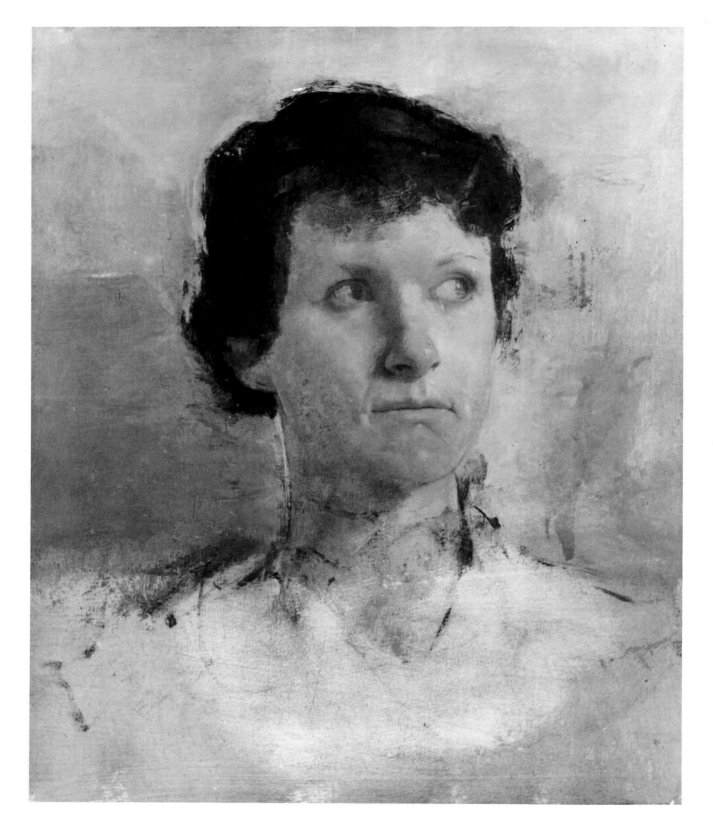

PORTRAIT OF SALLY BAGG
1959. Oil on cardboard, 8 × 10 in.
Private collection.

reflecting what was then current: abstract expressionism. The painting ended as a kind of scene emptied of all obvious representational references. When it was finished, I coated it with white lead and began another painting that became *Street Scene 1955–58*. There were no compositional studies for this painting. I painted for a long time without knowing the final scale of the figures. I did know that I wanted to make a frescolike painting. The picture, however, is not large, but it seemed large in the small space in which I was working. I worked on the picture for almost four years. In the conventional sense it is unfinished. While I worked on the picture it occurred to me that the scene I was depicting was happening on a vanishing point on the horizon and was being viewed through binoculars or a telescope. The space then is brought forward with little change of scale from front to back. The result is a tight, depthless space emphasizing the surface—which coincided with my interest in wall painting.

I stayed in the studio on Tenth Street only one year, leaving it for a small apartment on the top floor of a tenement on Fourth Street with hot water and heat. I now had everything necessary for my life—a part-time job and a place, though small, with good light in which to work. In the three years I lived on Fourth Street I worked mostly on five paintings: the street scene, a portrait of Ruben Eshkanian, a portrait of Henry Kowert playing a guitar, a still life with a white pitcher, and a painting of a Victorian boy from an old photograph. Except for painting from the photograph, these pictures were endlessly changing. Two were left incomplete. The Ruben portrait changed its size three times, finally being pasted down to make use of the canvas nailed to the stretcher. The problem stemmed, I think, from the fact that the backgrounds in these paintings were made up. This meant that I had endless possibilities—a freedom not necessarily to be desired. Degas and de Kooning wrestled with the same dilemma: deciding on the space the subject is to inhabit. Generally, I tend to go for more space, with the figures becoming smaller.

In 1958, after applying for the third time, I was awarded a fellowship to the American Academy in Rome.

Before leaving New York I took snapshots of storefronts and stoops. The Academy had large studios, I was told, and I wanted to try and paint something large using New York as a setting. Because I needed something to set off the action, I decided on an accident. Looking through my street paintings, there seems to be a theme of youth confronting life in an active way. Much of American painting in the forties treated children as a subject, but usually in a sentimental, often stylized, manner. I hated that. I liked the fresh note of Degas's youths in his *Spartan Boys and Girls at Play*—in fact, I divided my picture between male and female in a tribute to that abortive picture—and the modest, unheroic proportions of the figures in the Halicarnassus frieze. Squaring up a compositional sketch, I began immediately without drawings for the figures. For myself, I fear too much preparation. I did a number of drawings, but all while the painting was in progress. Rome itself inspired me; the ocher walls catching fire late in the afternoon. To catch this I had to adopt a new key. Before Rome, my pictures had been cool; from Rome on, they tended to be warm.

In 1959, visiting Greece, I began to paint landscapes, adopting, as I understood it, Edwin Dickinson's approach, that of painting a quick glance.

When I returned to America in 1961 I began teaching. As a starting point I decided to go back to Dickinson's teacher, Charles Hawthorne. I had read *Hawthorne on Painting* in high school and was attached to his view that nature is best approached through color relationships rather than drawing. I have given his idea my own start over the years, emphasizing value over color. Teaching has made a big difference in my work, I think. The rigors of responding to so many setups in each class could not help but make for a thinking eye.

I finally had my first exhibition—at the Tanager Gallery on Tenth Street in 1962. Looking at my work together, I decided to stop painting from my head.

STILL LIFE WITH PAPER PLATE AND BUN
1982. 6 × 10 in. Private collection.

STILL LIFE WITH ETRUSCAN POT
1975. Oil on canvas, 8 × 11 in. From the collection of Howard and Joanna Ross.

STILL LIFE WITH EARTHENWARE VESSEL
1973. Oil on canvas, 60 × 50 in. Collection of Bowdoin College Museum of Art, Brunswick, Maine.

The forms in my large street scene seemed flatter than in the previous one. I am sure my teaching was pulling me toward painting from direct observation. I call this "humble pie." Conceptual painting is "pie in the sky."

I worked from still lifes, single figures, and landscapes through the sixties. Gradually, however, what I was learning began to encourage me to think again of painting "pie in the sky." I was looking at Corot less and more at Giotto and other fresco painters.

In 1970 I began working on another street scene. I was inspired by a Pompeian painting of a street scene in which the characters are all looking away from each other. The atmosphere is electric with mistrust because it is clear everyone is aware of everyone else. My painting would be vertical this time, with only four figures and a dog and the composition on a slight diagonal. I had a terrible time painting the boy hanging off the post. No model could hold the pose and a photo was not feasible. Nailing a small stretcher on a door to hold on to and looking in a mirror, I began posing. Being at an angle myself made measuring an impossibility. Finally, after two years I thought of squaring off the mirror and squaring off my drawing paper. Wherever I crossed a line on the mirror I made a corresponding mark crossing the proper line on my paper. Then, connecting these intersections, I found I had a figure.

With this picture I freed myself of the dogmas of working from life or working from my imagination exclusively. Though I tend to work on one picture at a time, I don't feel I have to be true to one mode or to the other.

Someone has said that you spend your life learning what you knew in the first place. I have always considered myself essentially a tonal painter. That is, I tend to find a tone (basically a value) from which the other tones in the picture are found. This approximates what one sees in the motif (nature) and supports a conviction that one is painting what one sees. In *Still Life with Kettle,* however, I discovered how extremely limited the value range is in a painting as against that which occurs in nature. It is obvious when one thinks about it. After all, a painting is essentially one plane and will reflect the light that is falling on it. It can be darkened or lightened with paint, it is true, but the picture will always remain one plane, placed one way in relation to the light. Nature, however, has no such limitation. Light strikes the kettle here, slides by, and barely seeps under the paper plate there. It was my task to try to get the feeling of this vast range of tones on this one plane.

Tonal painting is naturally suited to simple surfaces usually closely related in terms of value and color, achieving a feeling of continuity and wholeness. One of the problems with tonalism, however, is that it is so difficult to deal with patterns. This is because patterns cannot be generalized and resist simplification. They are made up of equal voices and they must be treated as such. However, such passages lend a richness, a musical quality, so to speak, that I coveted for *Still Life with Popcorn Maker,* but not at the expense of tone.

In this still life I attempted two main patterns: one turned on the diagonal—red and white cloth on the table—and another on the horizontal—orange and brown linoleum on the wall. Into this very dissonant situation I mixed a popcorn maker, a brilliant red cloth, a white scalloped dish with a pomegranate, a chair, and other objects. It seemed to me this complexity reverberated as a whole even though each spot in it struck its own note. I tried to get this.

One afternoon in the middle fifties, I decided to

NUDE
1961–64. Oil on canvas, 50⅛ × 42 in.
Collection of The Brooklyn Museum.

STILL LIFE WITH POPCORN MAKER
1982. Oil on canvas, $15\frac{1}{8} \times 23\frac{15}{16}$ in.
Collection of Peter A. Blum.

STILL LIFE WITH KETTLE
1977. Oil on canvas, $46 \times 38\frac{1}{8}$ in.
Collection of The Cleveland Museum of Art.

LENNART ANDERSON

paint a little everyday picnic scene. I changed it soon after I began, when it occurred to me that I really wanted to paint a bacchanal. Probably there is an irony here—that I used an abstract expressionist attitude (change your painting in a flash) to paint the archetypal subject. The painting took perhaps an hour to paint. I wasn't sure what to think of it. It came so easily that I decided it wasn't mine. It was a gift from somewhere. My little bacchanal became my favorite picture. I packed it in the trunk when I left for Rome and hung it wherever I lived. It was a tongue-in-cheek version of a type of painting I loved above all others: Raphael's *Galatea*, Titian's companion pictures *Bacchus and Ariadne* and *The Andrians*, certain Poussins, and Ingres's wall painting *The Age of Gold*. I thought of it as a sketch for a painting I most wanted to do but never would. I couldn't dare such a fiasco. The nude figure in action? Sunlight? Water? Landscape?

By the late seventies, after so much time teaching from the model, I knew I must try it. Stretching three large canvasses, I decided to paint with acrylics. I knew these paintings would probably be endlessly revised, and though I hadn't painted with plastic, I knew that medium could be worked over and over without endangering its permanence. Also, I liked the idea of a water-based paint lending the lighter key of fresco. My only chance for success, I felt, was to set an amiable tone and to maintain it. To think of the painting as something effervescing and not final.

I started the first picture by reversing the sketch, hoping that new material would naturally occur. The second painting was taken directly from the sketch, and the third (still being worked on) was based on a combination of the first two paintings with some new ideas.

I finally settled on *Idylls* as a title for these pictures.

This freed them from any iconographic responsibilities that attach to *Bacchanal* or *Arcadia*. I had included a little toy steamboat in the original sketch to deliberately frustrate any attempt to place this scene in ancient times. Titian did a similar thing when he included women in contemporary dress in *The Andrians*. Matisse comes to mind when thinking of more recent attempts at such a subject. His *Lux, Calme et Volupté* has no overt contemporary clues. Style alone makes it clear it is a modern picture.

I conceived of these pictures as passive decorations—pictures that stay on the wall and seduce only if one is of a mind to be seduced. I like to think of them shaded by some loggia near a swimming pool with wet pavement, plants, and sunlight.

I do my best. I am anxious not to fool myself. If my work is received with pleasure, I am gratified. If not, I can't help it.

Looking back, I think the direction I took in 1951 had more to do with criticism of the representational painting being done in America at that time than it did with abstraction. The painting that has meant the most to me has always had its elements of realism without necessarily being characterized as such: Titian and Ingres spring to mind. It is the tactile identification of paint with form that is satisfying to me. That is a long way from the abject realism that is around today, however. Nature resists being copied; it flattens and dries out under that approach. I have learned that I must be prepared to be surprised if I'm going to approach nature in its lair. It continually surprises me. For me as a painter, nature is not an apple, but how an apple is seen in its surroundings. Nature has a way of making liaisons between even very disparate elements, and it is my delight when I discover how it accomplishes this.

BACCHANAL
1955–56. Oil on canvasboard, 16 × 20 in.
Collection of the artist.

LENNART ANDERSON

157

IDYLL I
1978–81. Acrylic on canvas, 68 × 84 in.
Courtesy Davis & Langdale Company, Inc.

IDYLL II
1979–80. Oil on canvas, 64⅛ × 80⅞ in.
Courtesy Davis & Langdale Company, Inc.

LENNART ANDERSON

Louisa Matthiasdottir

I was born in Iceland. My parents were interested in painting and encouraged me to study it. They sent me to art school in Copenhagen, then to study with Marcel Gromaire in Paris. When the war came I couldn't continue my studies in Europe so I came to New York and studied with Hans Hofmann in his school in Greenwich Village.

I try to go back to Iceland at least once a year. My husband and I share an apartment in Reykjavik with our daughter. When I go back, I do a great deal of painting and sketching directly from the landscape. I guess when one is born somewhere or is young in a particular place one knows that part of the world better than any other and is more attached to it than any other. So it seems natural that I should want to paint Iceland. Its atmosphere is very clear. It doesn't have the sort of haze that one finds in other parts of Europe. Here in America there are days similar to those in Iceland, extremely bright days with very sharp, almost hard, light. These are, of course, the good days. When it's raining, days everywhere are the same. Most people say Iceland must be like Maine, but that is true only of parts of Iceland. Because Iceland is volcanic, it has many more colors. The lava is red and black and there are glaciers; one doesn't see such colors in Maine. One of the characteristics of Iceland that I like is the fact that there are no trees to speak of. When there are trees one doesn't really see beyond them, one can't get a sense of the horizon. In Iceland, the landscape is unobstructed, allowing one to see for great distances.

As to painting, I start painting and that's about it. I don't say, "Well now I'll do it this way," and then try to do it. I just look. I look at the landscape and then do what I feel. Of course, I have to decide if I'm going to use this color or that color, this form or that form, but so does anyone who paints.

In the studio, I set up still lifes, then I paint them, sticking to what is there. I don't put in a potato that's not there or anything of that sort. Of course, when I do landscapes from memory that is a different matter. I may add a sheep here, a house there, as the painting demands.

I paint all day, more or less. Sometimes I'll make a drawing first, sometimes not. I paint quickly, but I must concentrate completely when I paint.

FISHING PARTY
1972. Oil on canvas, 59 × 70¼ in.
Private collection.

ICELANDIC VILLAGE
1977. Oil on canvas, 44 × 52 in.
Collection of the artist.

LOUISA MATTHIASDOTTIR

HONEY JAR
1978. Pastel on paper, 12 × 19 in.
Collection of Robert and Ginny Stoppenbach.

KISA
1978. Pencil on paper, 8½ × 5½ in.
Collection of the artist.

GIRL WITH SHEEP
1977. Oil on canvas, 50 × 50 in.
Collection of the artist.

LOUISA MATTHIASDOTTIR

MAN ON HORSEBACK
1979. Oil on canvas, 18 × 22 in.
Collection of the artist.

LOUISA MATTHIASDOTTIR

ESJA
1980. Watercolor, 7 × 10¼ in.
Collection of the artist.

I do a lot of paintings and I enjoy doing them, but I don't know if I learn anything from them. I'm probably like all other painters; I don't even know what determines the size of a painting. I might go to the easel and think, "Well, I have only so much time. I'll do a little painting." Or I'll decide I have a lot of time and then do a large one. It's as simple as that.

One never knows any landscape so well that one doesn't want to paint it anymore. Besides, one always falls short of what is actually there. Whether I'm painting in the studio without a model or landscape in front of me, or painting directly from a landscape or still life, everything goes wrong if the forms don't adjust themselves on the canvas. At times one paints and

LOUISA MATTHIASDOTTIR

168

feels that a lot of progress is made no matter what the subject. I go by what looks right in the painting. That's always the thing. Because if it doesn't look right in the painting it doesn't look like the subject, either.

The reason I paint is because I want to paint what I see. But to paint what I see I must build from color. I try to paint what I see. I don't do shapes and colors without seeing them in nature. Either it looks like a landscape or it doesn't. That's all. And also, either a form fits in the painting or it doesn't. After all, a painting isn't really a still life or a landscape, it's a mere canvas. It can never be real life. It has to be a painting.

REYKJAVIK HARBOR
1980. Watercolor, 7 × 10¼ in.
Collection of the artist.

RÁNARGATA
1982. Oil on canvas, 20 × 30 in.
Collection of the artist.

SELF-PORTRAIT WITH BROWN COAT
1980. Oil on canvas, 68 × 33 in.
Collection of the artist.

LOUISA MATTHIASDOTTIR

171

MOUNTAINS BY THE SEA
1980. Watercolor, 7 × 10¼ in.
Collection of the artist.

ICELANDIC LANDSCAPE
1981. Watercolor, 7 × 10¼ in.
Collection of the artist.

LOUISA MATTHIASDOTTIR

STILL LIFE WITH MORTAR AND PESTLE
1981. Oil on canvas, 38¼ × 58 in.
Collection of the artist.

TOMATOES WITH EGGPLANT AND BROWN GLASS
1980. Oil on canvas, 16 × 19 in.
Collection of Mr. and Mrs. H. J. Wehrli.

LOUISA MATTHIASDOTTIR

COMPOTE WITH FRUIT
1983. Pastel on paper, 12 × 19 in.
Collection of the artist.

SELF-PORTRAIT
1982. Pastel on paper, 19 × 12½ in.
Collection of the artist.

SELF-PORTRAIT
1983. Pastel on paper, 26 × 20¼ in.
Collection of the artist.

REYKJAVIK HARBOR
1981. Oil on canvas, 34 × 48 in.
Collection of The Continental Company, New York.

HOUSE AND SHEEP
1982. Oil on canvas, 33 × 52 in.
Private Collection, New York.

Wayne Thiebaud

I started drawing at sixteen, when I broke my back doing sports. I'd always been interested in cartoons and that's what I drew. I didn't know anything about painting, didn't even know how one became a painter. When I began to read, and for some reason became interested in it, then painting did become fascinating, but from a totally removed state. I have a very romantic idea of it.

I worked in the Disney studios for a short time, got involved in labor agitation, and was canned along with a lot of other people. Then I worked doing sign jobs and in advertising agencies. Slowly I began to work more in layout, because that was more interesting to me, but I was still doing quite a bit of cartooning. I went to New York and sold cartoons to magazines and continued to do that for a long time. When I went into the army I wanted to become a pilot but first studied airplane mechanics and just worked on the line. And then one day I saw some guys making posters so I became an army artist. And that is what I remained most of the time I was in the service.

I read about painting and got interested in it, but I think the thing that thrilled me about the idea of being an artist was seeing a living example of what it meant to be one in the person of a guy named Robert Mallary. We both worked at the Rexall Drug Company; he was a typographer, I was a layout art director. I could see right away he was very bright. He hadn't been to college. He'd run off when he was fourteen, went to Mexico and worked with Siqueiros and Orozco. But what I really thought of becoming, and wanted to become, was a commercial artist. I had, and continue to have, a great regard for commercial artists. I thought I would be a designer, an art director, and was developing a career in that direction, but the more I got interested in layout and design, the more I was led to those examples in fine art from which they derived. The most interesting designs were influenced by Mondrian or Degas or Matisse. That revelation really transfixed me. I started drawing a lot and read continually about it and slowly decided—by that time I already had a family—that I was going to try to become a painter. So for a couple of years I did it on the side. Finally I decided to go back to school, back to college, and get a degree so I could teach in order to have time to paint.

CAKE
1970. Oil on canvas, 30 × 24 in.
Private collection.

CAKES
1967. Pastel, 10 × 12 in.
Collection of Allan Stone.

TV STILL LIFE
1971. Charcoal on paper, 22 × 30 in.
Collection of the artist.

TOWEL AND TOOTHBRUSH
1971. Charcoal on paper, 22 × 30 in.
Collection of the artist.

WAYNE THIEBAUD

My first paintings were rough approximations of cubism. I was influenced by people like Braque, Marin, Feininger, and, oddly enough, combined them with Rico Lebrun's paintings of the stations of the cross, a very Picassoesque series done in the late 1940s. I was trying to figure out what to do. The first time I ever exhibited was in the Los Angeles County Art Association with seven other people in a kind of young talent show. I was thrilled to death. The person who picked me out was Lorser Feitelson, who was then teaching at the art center.

I came to Sacramento and began teaching in a junior college—it seemed like I was teaching about eighty hours a week. I was entranced by teaching. The continuing confrontation with basic questions of all kinds continues to be a fascination for me. I started instructing at Sacramento City College, continuing to paint on the side. In addition to teaching, I worked fairly hard at painting, exploring various traditions. My paintings continued to be essentially cubistic, but I also

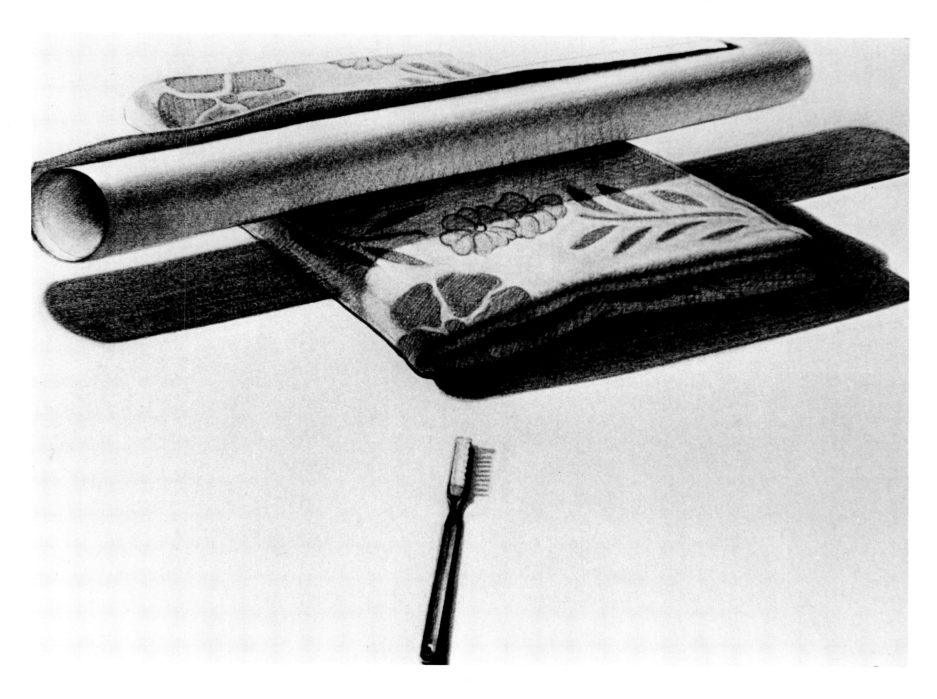

LYON & WASHINGTON
1974. Oil on canvas, 12 × 16 in.
Private collection.

GIRL IN PINK HAT
1974. Oil on canvas, approximately 32 × 24 in.
Private collection.

WAYNE THIEBAUD

NUDE ON HIGH STAND
1978. Charcoal on paper, 30 × 22 in.
Collection of the artist.

became more and more interested in the New York school, especially Willem de Kooning and the abstract expressionists. My problem was that I was also very interested in painting from the object, or working representationally, and I tried to hide that. I told myself, "You shouldn't paint an object, you shouldn't show an object," so I lavishly overlayered with all kinds of abstract expressionist brushstrokes. I did that continually through the early fifties. Then I began to be interested by very common objects, things in windows and on counters: gumball machines, pinball machines, jukeboxes, gambling machines. But my painting was still quite overworked with abstract expressionist mannerisms. About that time I also became influenced by the West Coast figurative school, people like Diebenkorn, Bischoff, Oliveira, Wonner. Plus there was a fascinating Spanish painter that attracted me by the name of Joaquin Sorolla. Tom Hess called him the John Singer Sargent of Spain. Very lavish and opulent brushwork and bravura, premier-coup painting. I got some books on him and did some works very much after him: boys on the beach, objects on counters. I was interested, I think, in the aspect of fractured light. Light that has direction, bounce, double reflection, suffusion, vibrations.

Then at the end of 1959 or so I began to be interested in a formal approach to composition. I'd been painting gumball machines, windows, counters, and at that point began to rework paintings into much more clearly identified objects. I tried to see if I could get an object to sit on a plane and really be very clear about it. I picked things like pies and cakes—things based upon simple shapes like triangles and circles—and tried to orchestrate them. Working from memory, I tried to arrange them in the same way that an art director arranges things. I wasn't that different from an art director except that I had more time, and I tried to be more careful, tried to be more refined and interesting in terms of relationships. My approach was very formalistic, except that I became increasingly affected by the idea of this odd subject matter. I didn't quite know why, but it seemed to me that there are certain objects that contain telltale evidence of what we're about as a people or as a society. But I wasn't interested in trying to explain or give answers so much as trying to present these objects so that they might be evocative in an existential sense. I tried to figure out why the object attracted me. A neutral description with a minimum of interpretation. I wanted to present it as directly as I could. A mimetic look after the object. The interesting problem with realism was that it seemed alternately the most magical alchemy on the one hand, and on the other the most abstract construct intellectually. Somehow the two had to merge. You can't depend, for instance, on a singular view of an object, at least I didn't feel I could, to dignify its presence or make it manifestly important unless it does something other than be a kind of replication, or simple visual recording.

Take, for instance, the energy of an overhead light. You can do one of two things—you can absolutely imitate its color and value patterns or you can, as Matisse does, create a system of color relations that create light itself; in other words, the picture creates its own light. That's an example of the kind of thing I mean about the abstracting of the object, translating it into a form, into the grammar of formal obligations of paintings, so that it can exist with a kind of respect on its own, as a single unique entity.

I remember painting pies—pumpkin pies—and I would try to keep them about actual size and put them on the plate and mix a sort of pumpkin color to see if I could create a dialectic between inert materials and visual phenomena. That was the idea and so I'd mix up this pumpkin color. I'd think, "What mixture of color makes a pumpkin? Orange-ocherish," and then I'd put it down as a slab, thinking, "Well, I want to also give it enough texture so that it has a kind of immediacy, a kind of pumpkin reality, otherwise it would look just like a slab of mud, a dead piece of nothing." I realized you can't mix colors that look like one thing or another; they have to be enlivened by a structural phenomenon of some kind if they are to come alive. I began drawing with oranges and colors sequentially

FLOWERED BLOUSE
1981. Charcoal on paper, 30 × 22 in.
Collection of the artist.

CHERRIES
1982. Pastel on paper, 18 × 21 in.
Collection of the artist.

FLAG
1971. Oil on canvas, 12 × 8 in.
Collection of the artist.

around the outside of the pumpkin pie, lighter and darker as a sort of system. Then I began to see what a little piece of red and a little piece of blue would do. As if one were setting pieces of mosaics into the paint.

You can enliven a construct of paint by doing any number of manipulations and additions to what one sees. This makes it possible for representational painting to be both abstract and real simultaneously. For example, when I talked earlier about pumpkin-pie colors, I should have said that it seemed like I painted shadows in a way that they might appear—and they just seemed to die. But if you stare at a strongly cast shadow, particularly in strong light like neon in window display counters, the two views that you see are not quite perfectly matched. Under strong light you get a vibration, which results from a breakdown of merger between the two separate eye views, and metaphorically you can represent that in a lot of ways. I think van Gogh used lime-green lines that would change to orange around edges of objects because he was experiencing objects under very strong light sources: incandescent light bulbs and the sun. My intention was to do something along that line. That is, to figure out a way to make an object look more alive, like it was glowing. The blues or the greens or the purples that I used were an attempt to do that.

My work does seem to change, but it's a cyclic change in a number of ways. It's a tightrope walk between the development of a convention that seems to answer a problematic demand and the need to avoid a formula that devitalizes the work by repetition and prejudice. Or how can a painter refresh himself by staying open to genuine questions?

A serious question would be whether or not those formalistic conventions, even though you've "discovered" them yourself, are dangerous, are too convenient. It's one reason why I change my direction, try to change my investigation from thing to thing. Actually, there is not much choice; it'll work or it'll just say right away, "Well, this is too disingenuous, it doesn't have enough passion, it doesn't have enough conviction." For instance, the objects and still lifes are all

done from memory but the figures, I realized at that time, couldn't be done from memory. Someone had to pose. Well, that presented a whole set of different problems for me, and when I did landscapes that was another set of problems. I combined painting directly from nature with memory.

I see myself as a very influenced painter. I really love art history and am thrilled by other painters, and I'll take directly, without any compunction about doing so, from painters I think I can use. I use art history as an inspirational wellspring and a sort of bureau of standards. Back to very basic concerns, back to provable, tangible results of that long tradition of the language of knowing things through painting and the inquiries around the grammar of painting.

Art history in its essence is an organic, growing, and changing discipline. It's more like a private game refuge, a treasure of exotic and wonderful rare Art Beasts. And our interests continue to change as we find out more and more. It's hard for me to recognize something like progress or evolutionary development, say in the Darwinian sense, in the development of art. For instance, though I've conscientiously studied his paintings for many years, I just can't find anything new, conceptually, in Paul Cézanne. For me he's just a damn good painter, who's used practically every device, convention, and trick in a painting, but he was so terrific, so bright, so careful in trying to be true to his relationships, that the painting is different, not because of any invention, despite his beliefs, but because of the composite structure and complexity of his perceptions translated into paintings.

What is interesting to many painters I know and respect is the sense of an unending community in the long tradition of painting. As an example of this, Cézanne rearranges objects or people or things to his "feel." He'll fuss and fool, finding an arm looks better here than it would have there, and each time he'll give you all the agony that goes with it. Ingres will too; he'll saw the arm off and just move it down there because it looks and feels better. As far as I am concerned, Ingres is as cubist as Picasso. I still think

WORKMAN
1982. Charcoal on paper, 30 × 22 in.
Collection of the artist.

SEATED FIGURE
1970. Charcoal on paper, 30 × 22 in.
Collection of the artist.

cubism came as much from Ingres as it did from Picasso, in that sense. And no one is the loser or winner, but each is an interesting variation, helping to sum up or anthologize human consciousness.

A problem, any problem in painting, if pursued, leads to an intellectual clarification of the notion of extremes. And a desire and need for critical development and evaluation. This is why critical awareness from other working artists, my peers, so mandatory. I owe a debt in this instance to someone like Robert Mallary, who was the most structured, formal, difficult, demanding critic that I've ever known. He had a terrific analytic mind—because not only would he find what seemed to be wrong in a picture but he would anticipate hypothetically eight different solutions and then turn the solutions on their heads.

FALL RIVER
1969. Oil on canvas, 40 × 40 in.
Private collection.

DRESSED WOMAN
1982. Oil on canvas, 30 × 24 in.
Courtesy Allan Stone Gallery.

SARDINES
1964. Pastel, 12 × 9½ in.
Private collection.

FREEWAY TRAFFIC
1976. Graphite on paper, 22 × 30 in.
Private collection.

It was astounding. I find I'm very interested in a critical means to help sharpen distinctions and discriminations. But if there is a great lack in modernism it would be the the lack of a critical community to provide the artist with confrontation of sufficient depth and seriousness. The idea of an art doctor appeals to me, someone to help straighten out your color or improve your composition.

Most of us, most painters, certainly myself, could use much more editing, much more confrontation of fact in terms of what our work is about. It might open up possibilities for endless change.

NIGHT DOWNGRADE
1981. Oil on canvas, 60 × 48 in.
Collection of the artist.

FREEWAY CURVE
1982. Oil on canvas, 31 × 29 in.
Private collection.

WAYNE THIEBAUD

Neil Welliver

When I finished the Philadelphia Museum College, I tried to paint on my own and find a job to support my painting. I tried advertising drawings for about six months and that was disastrous; an easy way to make money, but a dead end. Then I taught in a public school until the loyalty-oath came along. I couldn't sign it, so I left. Then I saw some of Albers's paintings. I saw one of those really vibrant ones, and I knew damn well I was in the presence of something I'd never seen before. I talked about it to a friend of mine who said, "He teaches at Yale. You should go there." I went to New Haven and met Albers. I did not go there with a decent body of student work. I'd been out of art school a year or two and was scratching around, making small drawings, trying to figure out some way to make pictures. I went there with drawings, and Albers said, "The stuff's terrible. The stuff's absolutely awful that you've brought me." I also brought him some sculpture I was working on—clay. He said, "This stuff's awful, too. But I see something, so I'm going to try you." He was right about my work: I was dropping skills learned in school and trying to do something else. The stuff was pretty damn grim.

The first paintings I did at Yale were still the farm machinery I painted in college. Albers wasn't unfriendly toward them, but they weren't relevant to what was going on at Yale. I couldn't learn anything through them. Curiously, they were landscape-oriented—farm machinery sitting in a field with the horizon always there. Then I did totally abstract paintings, which subsequently became color field paintings. It was Albers's influence. He became angry with me when he saw me as a convert to hard reductive painting. But that was never the case. The paintings were a means through which I could learn what Albers had to teach about color. His anger grew when my painting became open. In some of my last pictures at Yale I even committed the crime of letting something drip onto them, and Albers was furious with me. But then he asked me if I wanted a job teaching with him and I said yes. It wasn't much of a job—the pay was terrible.

At that time Conrad Marca-Relli introduced me to Eleanor Ward, who expressed interest in my having a show of abstract pictures at the Stable Gallery. I decided not to do it because the paintings that interested Eleanor were the reductive abstract color field works. I didn't want to be stamped with that imprimatur.

VICKI
1973. Oil on canvas, 60 × 60 in. Collection of Mr. and Mrs. Martin Sosnoff.

NILE AND BOWSER
1967. Oil on canvas, 55½ × 45¾ in. Private collection, New York.

I thought if I got caught in the gallery network, development would end. I knew I was going to take my work somewhere else, I was going to paint or I wasn't, I was going to go my own way or I wasn't, and it was a direction other than where the art world was going. Nothing to be done but to ride it out.

I had two of the worst years of my life after that. I couldn't do anything. I was trying to lay everything aside and be a child again. Everyone goes through that in some form or another. If you become conscious of what you're doing, which is trying to find the first steps on a path you want to take, I think you have a tendency to try to unload all your baggage and walk as a child. Of course, you reclaim some of the baggage later. The stuff I was doing was terrible. I was on the floor with sand and pumice, trying all of the things that I had seen in modern painting but never tried. I needed to lay aside what was learned, to try to pick up what was not. Slowly I began to find things in painting. And a direction began to form. It came from cartoons, drawings from nature, art history, anything. My paintings were loose, wild, takeoffs on historical painting. I even redid the *Burial of Count Orgaz.*

One's vision of the world is part of the subject of one's painting, and my vision had been rural—I grew up in Pennsylvania in an environment that was unspoiled country woods and so on—and that vision slowly took over the paintings more and more and more. It was a scrambled time, painful and difficult, but it was not thrust upon me by fate; it was my decision.

I moved into painting figures and landscapes crudely. I went to French Canada. My first idea was to settle where I had some friends, but my French was appalling and I moved on. I worked my way down the Atlantic coast, and just beyond Augusta I began to think, "Gee, this looks right; this feels right, it's terrific."

Then I reached Lincolnville, a few miles from the ocean, a few miles from Belfast. Lois Dodd was there; Alex Katz was there. They had a cottage because they'd been to Skowhegan in summer school, and I stayed with them. I hit the back roads looking for land and a house. Found them. Been here ever since.

In Maine there is an extraordinary clarity. You can look for a mile but objects seem right before your face; you can identify them. I'm interested in the character of the light—that northern flat light—where the sun doesn't get very high. And in the relatively young land, a lot of it is geologically young. Great erratics are lying all over the place, great granite boulders. The upheaval is still apparent, the gouging of the glaciers, all of that. It didn't happen very long ago; it is evident. Still, it's not the drama of the landscape that attracts me at all, because I paint what would, in terms of theater, be considered innocuous and banal—ordinary places. I could paint in places other than Maine. But I could not paint where the landscape doesn't interest me, where it's not complicated enough, where it's been too ordered by people.

When I look now at historical painting, nineteenth-, twentieth-century landscapes, they appear unreal, even those favorite painters of mine. Only very rarely do I see something that seems to me complete. When I see a Courbet or a Corot it seems empty. I mean no derogation of the painters. But I want something more that I haven't found in any other painter. The Hudson River pictures look to me procedural, systematic, structured, controlled, and prefabricated.

What interests me is to walk into the woods and turn in any direction and suddenly see something that strikes me, something that's absolutely staggering. When I do, I hang out there, going back, walking and walking through the same area again and again. The picture I'm working on now I started eight years ago.

THREE WOMEN WITH SKELETONS
1955. Watercolor, 21 × 21 in.
Private collection.

NEIL WELLIVER

SALT FLAT
1971. Oil on canvas, 48 × 48 in. Private collection, Boston.

NEIL WELLIVER

BEAVER DAM
1971. Oil on canvas, 60 × 60 in. Private collection, Boston.

NEIL WELLIVER

I just hung around that stream. I go back there all the time and to that very area, back and forth, and I look and look, and then I see something there and paint it. Now what is seen is very difficult to describe. That's a metaphysical issue. I've taken the camera and taken photographs—I don't use photographs in my work and they have nothing to do with what I see there. I've been hanging around that spot on that little brook for eight years. There's incredible archetypal stuff right there. It's a great granitic outcropping that comes right up out of the earth; the ice has heaved it, it's been split, cracked, broken up, there are boulders around, and then abruptly the surface changes, and there's all this organic material growing over it. It's a primal spot. It's not just a brook but a place where elemental forces are revealed.

There's something interesting in the Castaneda books. The main character, Don Juan, talks about places of power. People go to them because that's what they are. Each one is the locus of some contact that one has with another world. I find if you paint and get involved in a place—none of these are great theatrical views—and study it and develop some understanding of it and hence affection for it, then the place becomes unbelievably particular. And there is no generality anymore. Generalities are wiped out of your life. But you discover that you were educated to deal with generalities. So that part of your intelligence gets laid aside and suddenly you are a device through which material can move, a position that would never have been possible for you in any formal situation because you wouldn't allow it. That's the excitement of painting.

Particularity is extraordinarily important, central to my work. But that particularity cannot be gotten by merely recording. It has nothing to do with putting down everything you see. It's a particularity that has to do with, one would hope, primal qualities.

That's what I really dislike about Church and Cole, Cole in particular. He had a procedure for painting spruce trees. Scumble, color, scumble. Chug-a-chug-a-chug-a-chug. He could put in a thousand spruce trees in a day; and they're really like an idea of a spruce tree, not a spruce tree observed and understood. That doesn't interest me at all. I don't have a catalog of marks at all. Sometimes when the painting gets stuck I'll say, "Oh, shit, the last time I painted a tree I got it; I did it like that." But it never works twice.

I find the woods inexhaustible, overwhelming, really. I find them reducing other possibilities just by their presence. I meander in the woods. There's something devastating about walking through a spot that you've been through fifty times and suddenly seeing it. It forces itself on you. That's an incredible experience that is difficult, if not impossible, to make sense of.

I think about my painting a lot, but there's a point at which it becomes mysterious. I do it, and I don't really know what the hell's going on. There are so many strange things involved. For instance, the forest moves in a certain way. You can go out, and there will be the slightest breeze, or it will be still or very windy. There's a kind of motion that's dictated by the wind and other forces. And suddenly an animal will move. And you'll see that he's not subject to the dictated motion of the forest, because he has the stuff to resist it, to go against it. That's very exciting. And suddenly there's a curious separation of that which is influenced and that which controls its own direction, like a deer.

I was painting in one place where there were two deer hanging around. They were curious. (I'm very quiet so I see lots of animals.) They hung around on that ridge, most of the summer. Finally I made some paintings of them because they were bathed with the same light and their color related very much to colors in the forest; they became a gray color toward fall.

MAN WITH TWO WOMEN
1959. Watercolor, 31 × 22¾ in.
Private collection, New York.

POND PASS
1974. Oil on canvas, 96 × 96 in. Collection of Federal Reserve Bank of Boston.

NEIL WELLIVER

TO SI'S HILL
1974. Oil on canvas, 96 × 96 in. Collection of Federal Reserve Bank of Boston.

And yet the thing that distinguished them was their motion, which went against the natural motion of the forest. They moved absolutely. And that's why if you're alert when you're in the woods, you'll always see an animal, because he moves against what you know to be, in some complete and whole way, the forces that are at work there. That still interests me greatly, and it's not often been done. The last time it was done, outside of my deer paintings, which I think are good pictures, was by Courbet. Winslow Homer is part of the fur-fish-and-game tradition. He's interested in an animal as a trophy or a carcass or something like that, but not as a counterforce in nature. You know, you can bend all the trees in one direction, but that's not how you get motion in a canvas. You've got to do it in ways that are obscure, I think.

People have asked me why I stopped painting figures. I stopped painting people abruptly when it became clear to me that people are just a part of nature—at the same time, they are a distraction. They are so specific and so much a point of focus for myself as well as viewers; I am more interested in developing a structural organism. People ask me about it. I think about it a lot. I see the possibilities but right now I'm not interested in them. I don't want to edit my original impulse. I'm after the big form, the *totus porcus*—the whole hog.

I usually paint the small pictures outside in three-hour stretches over three or four days. I find that after three hours or so the light drifts away. The geometry is just too complicated to move in your head. I'll say, "Oh well, that happened five minutes ago." If it were physically possible to get the damn painting in and out, I would paint a big one outside. But it's a physical problem.

One day I painted outside on a large canvas, starting in the morning, about nine o'clock. By noon the light was getting pretty high and it was time to quit. I said, "I think I'll go on with it." I paint from top to bottom in my paintings and every day I finish just so much of it. Very unconventional way to paint. But it's helpful because when you reach the bottom you're finished. There's no going back. Anyway, by noon it was time to go on to something else, and I said, "No, I think I'll just paint." So I painted—painted till six o'clock. So that particular painting has three different lights in it, and they're all on that one canvas. Now there's a lot of that going on in my paintings. It's no great invention, except the thing that's interesting about it is that the mind will tolerate it, will tolerate a span of time and change in a single image. Rousseau did it. Rousseau's is the only work I've ever seen that did that.

I'm fond of Rousseau. Very fond of Rousseau, of his passion and intensity. If he paints a leaf, he begins with green and so much white at one end and then he reduces it, and it falls over a form, and the leaf becomes dark that way. Absolutely regular. Systematic. There is a kind of incredible stubbornness about it. Not in the Germanic sense of thinking you're right, but just knowing that that's the way things are, and so if you do it that way then you'll get a handle on it. I like that. I'm interested in him, but actually I like painting in general, and as one gets older one's preferences are less influenced by one's own work. One is excited by more and more things. Velázquez interests me, the execution of his paintings is so wild that I cannot learn from them in any specific sense. They're too exotic, too brilliant. But I love to look at them whenever I can.

CORNELIUS O'LEARY, BISHOP OF PORTLAND, MAINE
1976. Oil on canvas, 24 × 20 in.
Collection of the La Salle College Art Museum, Philadelphia.

NEIL WELLIVER

ANONYMOUS FRESHET
1975. Oil on canvas, 72 × 72 in.
Collection of Graham Gund.

BIG ERRATICS
1977. Oil on canvas, 94¼ × 120⅛ in.
Collection of Hirshhorn Museum and Sculpture Garden,
Smithsonian Institution.

NEIL WELLIVER

215

I make a large drawing from the small drawings and paintings, and then I puncture a large sheet of paper, the actual size of the canvas, with a sewing needle and transfer it to the canvas. That makes what I am putting down extremely general. It generalizes a drawing, places things. Then the description is done when I paint. The painting is made then. I take great liberties after the drawing, liberties in the name of intensity.

I choose my color the same way. I've been using the same eight colors for about ten years. They're basic. No earth tones. But sometimes I take liberties. For instance, I've been painting some autumn paintings this year and I discovered that all those curious aniline-dye reds that you find in "autumn art" can't be made with the cadmium red scarlet that I use, so I've added deep cadmium, a color close to rose madder.

When I finish painting in the late afternoon I can hardly stand up. I'm so exhausted. I paint seven hours in the studio and there's little procedure involved in my painting. There's no scumbling, there's no scraping, nothing. The paintings are prime. Every time I touch a canvas I make a form, so when I talk about seven hours of painting I'm talking about at least six hours of really touching the canvas. And I work on only one at a time, I can't work on two. It may be a weakness. I have to garner all my energies and focus them to work. The way I paint is totally focused and intense and complete—every mark is a form that's not going to be covered up later. I don't revise anything. I don't go back. I don't go over it. I go down the canvas to the bottom and out, and that's it. I never go back. There's no rethinking. The changes that are made are made by adjusting what happens there with what you do here, not by going back. When things don't suit me, I just abandon them. Sometimes I abandon them altogether, sometimes for a period of time and come back to them. But they don't smell right when they're not working. They have a bad odor. You can tell.

Sometimes whatever it is that can be made clearer in a larger picture isn't present in a small one. Sometimes a small picture is what it is and that's that. It doesn't want to be large and you know it; making it larger isn't going to do anything for it. So you leave it. That happens roughly half the time to me. For me the real problem with scale is that of trying to seduce a person into really feeling that he can walk into your canvas. And eight feet seems big enough and much bigger doesn't add anything to it. But a much smaller size will cut people out. I hope the viewer is sucked in there as into a vacuum. On occasion, someone will say to me, usually someone who isn't very sophisticated about pictures, "Oh, I just wanted to walk right in there." And that is not dumb. The person is saying, "I was really drawn to be there, in that place," and for me that's one of the most touching comments I can get about a painting.

Fairfield Porter came to my place one time, and it was the first time he'd ever seen a painting of mine in progress; the upper part was finished and the lower part empty canvas. He said, "That simply can't be done, can't be done." And I said, "But, Fairfield, I'm doing it." And he said that he didn't like it. It made him feel uncomfortable. Sometime later we were talking about it and he said, "You think differently. I can see the possibility, but you have to use your mind very differently than I use mine." And I do use my mind differently. Otherwise everyone would be painting this way.

STUDY FROM WOOD DUCK
1976. Pencil and watercolor on paper, 9¾ × 7½ in.
Courtesy Marlborough Gallery, New York.

NEIL WELLIVER

FROZEN SPRING
1974. Oil on canvas, 96 × 96 in. Collection of Leslie and Stanley Westreich.

SHADOW
1977. Oil on canvas, 96 × 96 in. Collection, The Museum of Modern Art, New York.

NEIL WELLIVER

STUDY FOR DROWNED CEDARS
1978. Pencil on paper, 8¼ × 10¾ in.
Courtesy Marlborough Gallery, New York.

STUDY FOR SPRUCE STAND
1980. Pencil on paper, 15¾ × 14½ in.
Courtesy Marlborough Gallery, New York.

STUMP
1974. Oil on canvas, 60 × 60 in. Collection of Dr. and Mrs. Richard Newman.

NEIL WELLIVER

DEER ON EAST BANK
1980. Oil on canvas, 96 × 96 in. Collection of Roselyne and Richard Swig.

NEIL WELLIVER

DRAWING FOR BURNT BARREN
1981. Pencil on paper, 22⅜ × 22⅛ in.
Courtesy Marlborough Gallery, New York.

STUDY FOR MEGUNTICOOK MOUNTAIN
1981. Pencil on paper, 14 × 16½ in.
Courtesy Marlborough Gallery, New York.

NEIL WELLIVER

AUTUMN BLUEBERRY BARREN
1982. Oil on canvas, 96 × 96 in. Collection of Leslie and Stanley Westreich.

LATE SPRING BROOK
1982. Oil on canvas, 96 × 96 in. Collection of Mr. and Mrs. Bruce C. Gottwald. Courtesy Marlborough Gallery, New York.

Chronologies

William Bailey

BIOGRAPHY

1930. Born in Council Bluffs, Iowa
1948–51. Studied at University of Kansas, School of Fine Arts
1951–53. Served in U.S. Army, Japan and Korea
1955. Received BFA from Yale University School of Art
1955–56. Studied in Rome
1957. Studied with Josef Albers and received MFA from Yale University School of Art
1962–69. Professor of Fine Arts, Indiana University, Bloomington
1965–66. Lived and worked in Paris
1969–78. Professor of Art, Yale University
1974–75. Dean of School of Art, Yale University
1976–77. Visiting Artist, The American Academy in Rome
1979–84. Kingman Brewster Professor of Art, Yale University

AWARDS

1955. Alice Kimball English Travelling Fellowship
1958. First Prize in Painting, Boston Arts Festival
1965. Guggenheim Fellowship in Painting. Ingram-Merrill Foundation Grant in Painting
1983. Meadows Distinguished Visiting Professor in Art, Southern Methodist University, Dallas, Texas

The artist lives and works in New Haven, Connecticut, and near Perugia, Italy. He is represented by Robert Schoelkopf Gallery, Ltd., New York.

ONE-MAN AND SELECTED GROUP EXHIBITIONS

1956. Robert Hull Fleming Museum, University of Vermont
1957. Kanegis Gallery, Boston, Massachusetts
1958. Kanegis Gallery, Boston, Massachusetts
1961. Kanegis Gallery, Boston, Massachusetts
1963. Indiana University Museum of Art, Bloomington
1967. Kansas City Art Institute, Kansas City, Missouri
1968. Robert Schoelkopf Gallery, New York
1969. Nasson College, Berwick, Maine
1970. Group exhibition: "22 Realists," Whitney Museum of American Art, New York; Norfolk Museum of Art, Virginia; Museum of Art, Ogunquit, Maine.
1971. Robert Schoelkopf Gallery, New York
1972. Tyler School of Art, Temple University, Philadelphia. Queens College, New York. University of Connecticut.
Group exhibition: "Five Figurative Artists," Kansas City Art Institute, Missouri; Weatherspoon Gallery, University of North Carolina, Greensboro; Butler Institute of American Art, Youngstown, Ohio.
1973. Galleria La Parisina, Turin, Italy. Galleria Dei Lanzi, Milan, Italy. Galleria Il Fante de Spade, Rome.
1974. Robert Schoelkopf Gallery, New York
1976. The Dart Gallery, Chicago
1978. Galerie Claude Bernard, Paris
1979. "Recent Paintings," Robert Schoelkopf Gallery, New York. "Still Lifes and the Figure," Barbara Fendrick Gallery, Washington, D.C.
Group exhibition: "American Painting of the 60s and 70s: The Real, The Ideal, the Fantastic," Whitney Museum of American Art, New York.
1980. Galleria d'Arte il Gabbiano, Rome
Group exhibition: "The Figurative Tradition," Whitney Museum of American Art, New York
1981. Group exhibitions: "The Whitney Biennial," Whitney Museum of American Art, New York. "Contemporary Artists," The Cleveland Museum of Art.
1981–82. Group exhibitions: "Real, Really Real, Super Real: Directions in Contemporary American Realism," San Antonio Museum of Art; Indianapolis Museum of Art; Tucson Museum of

Art; Museum of Art, Carnegie Institute, Pittsburgh. "Contemporary American Realism Since 1960," Pennsylvania Academy of the Fine Arts, Philadelphia; Virginia Museum of Fine Arts, Richmond; Oakland Museum, California. "American Painting, 1930–80," Haus der Kunst, Munich.

1982. "Recent Figure and Still Life Paintings," Robert Schoelkopf Gallery, New York. Group Exhibition: "A Heritage Renewed," University Art Museum, Santa Barbara, California.

1983. Meadows Gallery, Owen Art Center, Southern Methodist University, Dallas, Texas

PUBLIC COLLECTIONS

Arkansas Arts Center
William Benton Museum of Art, Connecticut
Des Moines Art Center
Duke University Art Gallery, Durham, North Carolina
General Mills Corporation, Minneapolis
Hirshhorn Museum and Sculpture Garden, Washington, D.C.
Kresge Art Center, Michigan State University, East Lansing
Lehman Brothers Kuhn Loeb, Inc., New York
Montclair Art Museum, Montclair, New Jersey
Museum of Art, Ogunquit, Maine
Museum of Art, Aachen, West Germany
Museum of Modern Art, New York
National Museum of American Art, Washington, D.C.
The New York Times, New York
Pennsylvania Academy of the Fine Arts, Philadelphia
Rose Art Museum, Brandeis University, Waltham, Massachusetts
St. Louis Museum of Art, Missouri
J. Henry Schroeder Banking Corporation, New York
J. B. Speed Museum, Louisville, Kentucky
State University of New York at Cortland
University of Kentucky, Lexington
University of Massachusetts, Amherst
University of Virginia Art Museum, Charlottesville
Weatherspoon Art Gallery, University of North Carolina at Greensboro
Whitney Museum of American Art, New York
Yale University Art Gallery, New Haven, Connecticut

Jack Beal

BIOGRAPHY

1931. Born in Richmond, Virginia
1950–53. Attended Norfolk division of the College of William and Mary/VPI (now Old Dominion University)
1953–56. Studied at the Art Institute of Chicago
1955–56. Studied at the University of Chicago
1975. *Portrait of Sydney and Frances Lewis* commissioned by Washington and Lee University, Lexington, Virginia
1976. Drawings commissioned by the U.S. Department of the Interior *The History of Labor in America* murals commissioned by the General Services Administration/U.S. Department of Labor

The artist lives and works in New York City and Oneonta, New York. He is represented by the Allan Frumkin Gallery, New York.

ONE-MAN AND SELECTED GROUP EXHIBITIONS

1965. Allan Frumkin Gallery, New York
Group exhibitions: "68th Annual Exhibition," Art Institute of Chicago. "Young America," Whitney Museum of American Art, New York.
1966. Allan Frumkin Gallery, Chicago
Group exhibition: "Neysa McMein Purchase Awards," Whitney Museum of American Art.
1967. Allan Frumkin Gallery, New York
1968. Allan Frumkin Gallery, New York
Group exhibitions: "National Invitational Exhibition," San Francisco Museum of Art. "Whitney Annual," Whitney Museum of American Art, New York.

1968–69. Group exhibition: "Aspects of a New Realism," Milwaukee Art Center, Wisconsin; Museum of Contemporary Art, Houston; Akron Art Institute, Ohio.
1969. Allan Frumkin Gallery, Chicago
Group exhibition: "Whitney Annual," Whitney Museum of American Art, New York.
1970. Allan Frumkin Gallery, New York
Group exhibition: "22 Realists," Whitney Museum of American Art.
1972. Allan Frumkin Gallery, New York. Miami-Dade Community College, Florida.
1973. Allan Frumkin Gallery, New York. Galerie Claude Bernard, Paris.
Group exhibition: "American Drawings, 1963–73," Whitney Museum of American Art, New York.
1973–74. "Retrospective Exhibition," Virginia Museum of Fine Arts, Richmond; Boston University; Museum of Contemporary Art, Chicago.
1974. Allan Frumkin Gallery, Chicago
Group exhibition: "Aspects of the Figure," Cleveland Museum of Art.
1975. Allan Frumkin Gallery, New York
1976–77. Traveling exhibition: Colorado State University, Fort Collins; University of Wyoming, Laramie; Fullerton College, California.
1976–78. Group exhibition: "America '76," organized by the U.S. Department of the Interior, and circulated to Corcoran Gallery, Washington, D.C.; Wadsworth Atheneum, Hartford, Connecticut; Institute of Contemporary Art, Boston; The Minneapolis Institute of Arts; Milwaukee Art Center; Fort Worth Art Museum; San Francisco Museum of Modern Art; The High Museum of Art, Atlanta; Brooklyn Museum.
1977. "Jack Beal: Prints and Related Drawings," Madison Art Center, Wisconsin; Boston University; Art Institute of Chicago.

1978. Allan Frumkin Gallery, New York
1979. Group exhibition: "Seven on the Figure," Pennsylvania
  Academy of the Fine Arts, Philadelphia.
1980. Allan Frumkin Gallery, New York. Reynolds/Minor Gallery,
  Richmond, Virginia.
1981–82. Group exhibitions: "Real, Really Real, Super Real:
  Directions in Contemporary American Realism," San Antonio
  Museum of Art; Indianapolis Museum of Art; Tucson Museum of
  Art; Museum of Art, Carnegie Institute, Pittsburgh.
  "Contemporary American Realism Since 1960," Pennsylvania
  Academy of the Fine Arts, Philadelphia; Virginia Museum of Fine
  Arts, Richmond; Oakland Museum, California.
1982. Galerie Claude Bernard, Paris.

PUBLIC COLLECTIONS

Art Institute of Chicago
Bruce Museum, Greenwich, Connecticut

Delaware Art Museum, Wilmington, Delaware
Minneapolis Institute of Art
Museum of Modern Art, New York
Neuberger Museum, Purchase, New York
Philadelphia Museum of Art
Philip Morris, Inc.
Ringling Museum of Art, Sarasota, Florida
Roby Foundation Collection
San Francisco Museum of Art
Toledo Art Museum, Toledo, Ohio
University of Notre Dame, South Bend, Indiana
University of Vermont, Burlington
University of Virginia Art Museum, Charlottesville
Valparaiso University, Valparaiso, Indiana
Wake Forest College, Winston-Salem, North Carolina
Walker Art Center, Minneapolis, Minnesota
Weatherspoon Art Gallery, University of North Carolina at
  Greensboro
Whitney Museum of American Art, New York

Jane Freilicher

BIOGRAPHY

1924. Born in Brooklyn, New York
1947. Received BA from Brooklyn College
1948. Studied with Hans Hofmann
1949. Received MA from Columbia University
1953. Drew illustrations for *Turandot and Other Poems* by John
  Ashbery
1975. Lithograph commissioned by The American Jewish Congress
  Paintings commissioned by the U.S. Department of the Interior for
  Bicentennial Exhibition, "America '76."
  Created book cover for Kenneth Koch's *The Art of Love*
1978. Created book cover for James Schuyler's *What's for Dinner*
1979. Designed set for Kenneth Koch's play *Red Robins*
1981. Designed set for John Ashbery's play *The Heroes*, Eye & Ear
  Theater Production
  Detwiller Visiting Artist, Lafayette College, Easton, Pennsylvania.

Jane Freilicher has been a visiting critic and lecturer at many schools
and universities including the University of Pennsylvania School of
Fine Arts, Philadelphia; Skowhegan School of Painting and
Sculpture, Skowhegan, Maine; Carnegie-Mellon Institute, Pittsburgh;
School of the Museum of Fine Arts, Boston; and the College of
Creative Studies, University of California at Santa Barbara.

AWARDS

1960. Selected by Alfred Frankfurter for the Hallmark Competition
1974. American Association of University Women Fellowship

1976. National Endowment for the Arts grant
1982. Elected to National Academy of Design

The artist lives and works in New York City and Watermill, Long
Island. She is represented by Fischbach Gallery, New York.

ONE-WOMAN AND SELECTED GROUP EXHIBITIONS

1952–72. Twelve exhibitions at the Tibor de Nagy Gallery, New York
1955. Group exhibitions: "Whitney Annual," Whitney Museum of
  American Art, New York. "Four Young Americans," Rhode Island
  School of Design, Providence.
1959. Group exhibition: "Recent Drawings, USA," Museum of
  Modern Art, New York
1963. Group exhibition: Museum of Modern Art, Hans Hofmann,
  New York
1964. Group exhibition: "Eight Landscape Painters," Museum of
  Modern Art, New York (traveled to Spoleto)
1966. Group exhibition: "Still Life Show," organized by the Museum
  of Modern Art, New York, and traveled to Spoleto, Italy.
1967. Group exhibition: "Landscapes," Smithsonian Institution,
  Washington, D.C.
1968. Cord Gallery, Southampton, New York
1971. John Bernard Myers Gallery, New York
1972. Benson Gallery, Bridgehampton, New York
1974. Benson Gallery, Bridgehampton, New York
1975. Fischbach Gallery, New York
1976–78. Group exhibition: "America '76," organized by the U.S.
  Department of the Interior, and circulated to Corcoran Gallery,

Washington, D.C.; Wadsworth Atheneum, Hartford, Connecticut; Institute of Contemporary Art, Boston; The Minneapolis Institute of Arts; Milwaukee Art Center; Forth Worth Art Museum; San Francisco Museum of Modern Art; The High Museum of Art, Atlanta; Brooklyn Museum.

1976–77. Wadsworth Atheneum, Hartford, Connecticut

1977. Fischbach Gallery, New York

1979. Fischbach Gallery, New York. Utah Museum of Fine Arts, University of Utah, Salt Lake City.

1980. Fischbach Gallery, New York

1981. Lafayette College, Easton, Pennsylvania.

1981–82. Group exhibitions: "Sunlight on Leaves: The Impressionist Tradition," Houston Museum of Fine Arts. "Real, Really Real, Super Real: Directions in Contemporary American Realism," San Antonio Museum of Art; Indianapolis Museum of Art; Tucson Museum of Art; Museum of Art, Carnegie Institute, Pittsburgh. "Contemporary American Realism Since 1960," The Pennsylvania Academy of Fine Arts, Philadelphia; Virginia Museum of Fine Arts, Richmond; Oakland Museum, California.

1982. College of the Mainland, Texas City, Texas. Watson/De Nagy Gallery, Houston.

1983. Fischbach Gallery, New York

PUBLIC COLLECTIONS

Amerada-Hess Corporation
American Federation of the Arts, New York
American Medical Association, Washington, D.C.
American Telephone and Telegraph Corporation
Ashland Oil Corporation
Becton-Dickson Corporation
Brooklyn Museum

Chase Manhattan Bank of North America
Citibank Corporation of North America
Commerce Bank of Kansas City
Continental Resources, Winter Park, Florida
Corcoran Gallery, Washington, D.C.
Crocker National Bank of California
Currier Museum of Art, Manchester, New Hampshire
Greenville Museum, Greenville, South Carolina
Guild Hall, East Hampton, New York
Hampton Institute, Hampton, Virginia
Hirshhorn Museum and Sculpture Garden, Washington, D.C.
Lehman Brothers
Main Hurdman Corporation, New York
Marion Koogler McNay Art Institute, San Antonio, Texas
Metropolitan Museum of Art, New York
Museum of Modern Art, New York
New York University
Parrish Art Museum, Southampton, New York
Prudential Insurance Company of America
Rahr-West Museum, Manitowoc, Wisconsin
R.C.A. American Communications, Inc., New Jersey
Reader's Digest
Rhode Island School of Design Art Museum, Providence
Rose Art Museum, Brandeis University, Waltham, Massachusetts
Simpson, Thatcher and Bartlett, New York
Stratford College, Stratford, Connecticut
Union Carbide Corporation
United Energy Resources, Texas
Utah Museum of Fine Arts, University of Utah, Salt Lake City
Weatherspoon Art Gallery, University of North Carolina at Greensboro
Westland Agency, Pennsylvania
Whitney Museum of American Art, New York

Philip Pearlstein

BIOGRAPHY

1924. Born in Pittsburgh, Pennsylvania

1949. Received BFA from Carnegie Institute of Technology, Pittsburgh

1955. Received MFA from New York University

1959–63. Instructor, Pratt Institute, New York

1962–63. Visiting Critic, Yale University, New Haven, Connecticut

1963–present. Professor of Art, Brooklyn College, New York

AWARDS

1958–59. Fulbright Fellow to Italy

1968. National Endowment for the Arts grant

1971–72. Guggenheim Fellowship in Painting

1973. National Academy of Arts and Letters

1982. Artist in Residence, American Academy in Rome

The artist lives and works in New York City. He is represented by Allan Frumkin Gallery, New York.

ONE-MAN AND SELECTED GROUP EXHIBITIONS

1955. Tanager Gallery, New York
Group exhibition: "Whitney Annual," Whitney Museum of American Art, New York

1956. Peridot Gallery, New York
Group exhibition: "Whitney Annual," Whitney Museum of American Art, New York

1957. Peridot Gallery, New York

1959. Tanager Gallery, New York. Peridot Gallery, New York.

1962. Allan Frumkin Gallery, New York. Kansas City Art Institute, Missouri.
Group exhibition: Society for Contemporary Art Exhibitions, Art Institute of Chicago.

1963. Allan Frumkin Gallery, New York

1965. Allan Frumkin Gallery, New York. Ceeje Gallery, Los Angeles. Reed College, Portland, Oregon.

1967. Allan Frumkin Gallery, New York. Bradford Junior College, Massachusetts.
Group exhibition: "Biennial Exhibition," Corcoran Gallery, Washington, D.C.

1968. Carnegie-Mellon University, Pittsburgh

1968–70. Group exhibition: "In a New Vein," organized by the Smithsonian Institution, traveled throughout Latin America.

1969. Allan Frumkin Gallery, New York
Group exhibition: "Aspects of a New Realism," Milwaukee Art Center; Houston Museum; Akron Art Institute.

1970. Chatham College, Pittsburgh
Group exhibition: "22 Realists," Whitney Museum of American Art, New York

1970–71. "Retrospective," Georgia Museum of Art, Athens; Wichita Art Museum, Kansas; Vassar College, Poughkeepsie, New York

1971. Graphics I and II Gallery, Boston

1971–72. Group exhibition: "Return to the Figure," Pennsylvania Academy of the Fine Arts, Philadelphia

1972. Galerie M. E. Thelan, Cologne, West Germany. Galleri Ostergren, Malmo, Sweden. Galerie Kornfeld, Zurich. Staatliche Museen, Kupferstichkabinett, Berlin. Kunstverein, Hamburg.

1972–73. Donald Morris Gallery, Detroit; Hansen Fuller Gallery, San Francisco; Parker 470 Gallery, Boston.

1973. Editions La Tortue, Paris
Group exhibitions: "Whitney Bi-Annual Exhibition," Whitney Museum of American Art, New York. "American Drawings," Whitney Museum of American Art, New York.

1974. Group exhibitions: "Twelve American Painters," Virginia Museum of Fine Arts, Richmond. "Selections in Contemporary Realism," Akron Art Institute, Ohio. "First International Biennial Exhibition of Figurative Painting," Tokyo, Japan. "Aspects of the Figure," Cleveland Museum of Art.

1974–75. "Prints and Drawings Retrospective," Finch College, New York; University of Texas at Austin; Cranbrook Academy, Bloomfield Hills, Michigan; Notre Dame University, South Bend, Indiana; Grand Rapids Art Museum, Michigan; Kalamazoo Institute of Arts, Michigan; Tampa Bay Art Center, Florida; Miami Art Center.

1975. Gimpel Fils Ltd., London. Neuberger Museum, State University of New York at Purchase. Marianne Friedland Gallery, Toronto. John Berger Gallery, Pittsburgh.
Group exhibition: "34th Biennial," Corcoran Gallery, Washington, D.C.

1976. Barbara Fendrick Gallery, Washington, D.C. Donald Morris Gallery, Detroit.

1977. Group exhibitions: "Nothing But Nudes," Whitney Museum Downtown, New York. "Eight Contemporary Realists," Pennsylvania Academy of the Fine Arts, Philadelphia; North Carolina Museum of Art, Raleigh.

1978–79. Harkus Krakow Gallery, Boston. "The Lithographs and Etchings of Philip Pearlstein," Springfield Art Museum, Missouri; University of Missouri, Kansas City; Civic Fine Arts Center, Sioux Falls, South Dakota; Madison Art Center, Wisconsin; Hunter Museum of Art, Chattanooga, Tennessee; University of Nebraska, Lincoln; Columbus Gallery of Fine Arts, Ohio; Scottsdale Center for the Arts, Arizona; Mint Museum of Art, Charlotte, North Carolina; Wesleyan University, Middletown, Connecticut; Boston University.

1979. Group exhibition: "Whitney Biennial," Whitney Museum of American Art, New York.

1980. Associated American Artists, New York
Group exhibition: "American Portrait Drawings," National Portrait Gallery, Washington, D.C.

1981. "Landscape Aquatints," Brooke Alexander, Inc., New York. Columbus College, Georgia. Ringling Museum, Sarasota, Florida. "Philip Pearlstein: Drawings and Watercolors," Reynolds/Minor Gallery, Richmond, Virginia.

1981–82. Group exhibitions: "Real, Really Real, Super Real: Directions in Contemporary American Realism," San Antonio Museum of Art; Indianapolis Museum of Art; Tucson Museum of Art; Museum of Art, Carnegie Institute, Pittsburgh. "Contemporary American Realism Since 1960," Pennsylvania Academy of the Fine Arts, Philadelphia; Virginia Museum of Fine Arts, Richmond; Oakland Museum, California.

PUBLIC COLLECTIONS

Ackland Art Museum, University of North Carolina at Chapel Hill
Akron Art Museum
Art Gallery, State University of New York at Albany
Art Institute of Chicago
Bloedel Collection, Williams College, Williamstown, Massachusetts
Brooklyn College
Brooklyn Museum
Brown University, Providence, Rhode Island
Canton Art Institute
Carnegie Institute, Pittsburgh, Pennsylvania
Cleveland Museum of Art
Colorado Springs Fine Arts Center
Corcoran Gallery, Washington, D.C.
Des Moines Art Center
Gibbs Art Gallery, Charleston, South Carolina
Grey Art Gallery, New York University
Hirshhorn Museum and Sculpture Garden, Washington, D.C.
Hunter College, New York
Indiana University Art Museum, Bloomington, Indiana
J. B. Speed Museum, Louisville, Kentucky
Johnson Museum, Cornell University, Ithaca, New York
Kalamazoo Institute
Metropolitan Museum of Art
Milwaukee Art Institute
Mitchener Collection, University of Texas at Austin
Museum of Contemporary Art, Chicago
Museum of Modern Art, New York
National Gallery, West Berlin
New Jersey State Museum, Trenton

Oklahoma City Arts Center
The Pennsylvania State University, University Park, Pennsylvania
Philadelphia Museum of Art
Princeton University
Randolph-Macon Women's College, Lynchburg, Virginia
Rensselaer Polytechnic Institute, Troy, New York
Reynolda House, Winston-Salem, North Carolina
Ringling Museum, Sarasota, Florida

Rose Art Museum, Brandeis University, Waltham, Massachusetts
San Antonio Museum of Art
Smart Gallery, University of Chicago
Spertus Museum of Judaica, Chicago
Toledo Museum of Art
University of Nebraska, Lincoln
Weatherspoon Art Gallery, University of North Carolina at Greensboro
Whitney Museum of American Art, New York

Alex Katz

BIOGRAPHY

1927. Born in Brooklyn, New York
1946–49. Studied at The Cooper Union Art School, New York
1949–50. Studied at Skowhegan School of Painting and Sculpture, Skowhegan, Maine
1960–63. Visiting critic, Yale University, New Haven, Connecticut

AWARDS

1972. Cooper Union Professional Achievement Citation
Guggenheim Grant in Painting
1980. St. Gaudens Medal in Art, The Cooper Union
Skowhegan Award in Painting

The artist lives and works in New York City. He is represented by Marlborough Gallery, New York, and the Robert Miller Gallery, New York (cut-outs).

ONE-MAN EXHIBITIONS

1954, 1957. Roko Gallery, New York
1959. Tanager Gallery, New York. Sun Gallery, Provincetown, Massachusetts.
1960–61. Stable Gallery, New York
1962. Tanager Gallery, New York. Martha Jackson Gallery, New York.
1964. Fischbach Gallery, New York. Grinnell Gallery, Detoit.
1965. Fischbach Gallery, New York
1966. David Stuart Gallery, Los Angeles
1967. Fischbach Gallery, New York
1968. Fischbach Gallery, New York. Bertha Eccles Art Center, Ogden, Utah. Towson State College, Baltimore.
1969. Phyllis Kind Gallery, Chicago. West Virginia University, Morgantown.
1970. Fischbach Gallery, New York
1971. Galerie Dieter Brusberg, Hanover, West Germany. Galerie Thelen, Cologne, West Germany. Phyllis Kind Gallery, Chicago. Fischbach Gallery, New York. Utah Museum of Fine Arts, University of Utah, Salt Lake City. "Alex Katz," originated by Utah Museum of Fine Arts, University of Utah, Salt Lake City, and

circulated to The Art Gallery, University of California at San Diego; Minnesota Museum of Art, St. Paul; Wadsworth Atheneum, Hartford, Connecticut.
1972. Reed College, Portland, Oregon. Sloan/O'Sickey Gallery, Cleveland.
1973. Carlton Gallery, New York. Assa Galleria, Helsinki, Finland. Marlborough Gallery, New York.
1974. Davison Art Center, Wesleyan University, Middletown, Connecticut. Marlborough Godard Gallery, Toronto and Montreal. "Alex Katz: Recent Works from the Collection of Paul J. Schupf," The Picker Gallery, Colgate University, Hamilton, New York.
1974–75. "Alex Katz Prints," originated by the Whitney Museum of American Art, New York, and circulated to Virginia Museum of Fine Arts, Richmond; Utah Museum of Fine Arts, University of Utah, Salt Lake City; Contemporary Graphics Center, The Santa Barbara Museum of Art; University Gallery, University of Minnesota, Minneapolis; Indianapolis Museum of Art.
1975. Marlborough Fine Art, London. Galerie Marguerite Lamy, Paris. Galerie Anesen, Copenhagen.
1976. Marlborough Gallery, New York. American Foundation for the Arts, Miami. Marlborough Godard Gallery, Toronto and Montreal.
1977–78. "Alex Katz: Some Recent Paintings," originated by Fresno Arts Center, California, and circulated to Long Beach Art Galleries, California State University; Seattle Art Museum; Art Gallery of Greater Victoria; Portland Center for the Visual Arts.
1977. Galerie Roger d'Amecourt, Paris. Marlborough Galerie, Zurich.
1978. Marlborough Gallery, New York. Mira Godard Gallery, Toronto and Montreal. Hokin Gallery, Chicago. Suzanne Hilberry Gallery, Birmingham, Michigan. Beaver College, Philadelphia. Rose Art Museum, Brandeis University, Waltham, Massachusetts.
1979. Brooke Alexander Gallery, New York. Suzanne Hilberry Gallery, Detroit. Robert Miller Gallery, New York.
1980. Queens Museum, Flushing, New York. Marlborough Gallery, New York.
1981. Suzanne Hilberry Gallery, Detroit. Mira Godard Gallery, Calgary and Toronto. Fay Gold Gallery, Atlanta. Hokin Gallery, Palm Beach, Florida. Birmingham Museum of Art, Birmingham, Alabama. Contemporary Arts Center, Cincinnati. Portland Center for the Visual Arts, Oregon. Robert Miller Gallery, New York.
1982. Marlborough Fine Art, London. Marlborough Gallery, New York. John C. Stoller and Company, Minneapolis. Hokin Gallery, Chicago.
1983. Marlborough Gallery, New York. Harkus Gallery, Boston.

Suzanne Hilberry Gallery, Detroit. McIntosh-Drysdale Gallery, Houston. Texas Gallery, Houston (cut-outs).

PUBLIC COLLECTIONS

Allen Memorial Art Museum, Oberlin College, Oberlin, Ohio
Art Institute of Chicago
Atheneum, Helsinki, Finland
Atlantic-Richfield Corporation, Los Angeles
Bayrische Staatbibliothek, Munich
Bowdoin College Art Museum, Brunswick, Maine
Chase Manhattan Bank, New York
Ciba-Geigy Art Collection, Ardsley, New York
Cleveland Museum of Art
Commerce Bank, University City, St. Louis, Missouri
Dartmouth College Museum, Hanover, New Hampshire
Delaware Art Museum, Wilmington, Delaware
Des Moines Art Center
Die Neue Galerie, Aachen, West Germany
Everhart Museum, Scranton, Pennsylvania
Fogg Art Museum, Harvard University, Cambridge, Massachusetts
Fort Worth Art Museum
Hayden Gallery and MIT Permanent Collection, Cambridge, Massachusetts
Helsinki Atheneum, Helsinki, Finland
Hirshhorn Museum and Sculpture Garden, Washington, D.C.
Institute of Arts, Detroit, Michigan
Israel Museum, Jerusalem
Madison Art Center, Madison, Wisconsin

Metropolitan Museum of Art, New York
Milwaukee Art Center
Museum of Art, Rhode Island School of Design, Providence
Museum of Fine Arts, Cincinnati
Museum of Modern Art, New York
National Collection of Fine Arts, Washington, D.C.
New Jersey State Museum, Trenton
New York University, New York
Pennsylvania Academy of the Fine Arts, Philadelphia
Philadelphia Museum of Art
Portland Museum of Art, Portland, Maine
Prudential Life Insurance Company, Newark, New Jersey
Rice University, Houston
Rose Art Museum, Brandeis University, Waltham, Massachusetts
Schroder Trust Company, New York City
Staatliche Museum, West Berlin
Syracuse University, Syracuse, New York
Tamayo Museum, Mexico City
Tokyo Gallery, Tokyo, Japan
University of Georgia, Athens
University of Iowa, Iowa City
University of Kansas, Lawrence
University of Southern California, Tampa, California
Utah Museum of Fine Art, Salt Lake City
Virginia Wright Fund, Seattle, Washington
Wadsworth Atheneum, Hartford, Connecticut
Wake Forest University, Winston-Salem, North Carolina
Weatherspoon Art Gallery, University of North Carolina at Greensboro
Whitney Museum of American Art, New York
Wichita Art Museum, Wichita, Kansas

Lennart Anderson

BIOGRAPHY

1928. Born in Detroit, Michigan
1946–50. Studied at and received BFA from Art Institute of Chicago
1950–52. Studied at and received MFA from Cranbrook Academy, Bloomfield Hills, Michigan
1961–62. Taught at Chatham College, Pittsburgh
1962–68. Taught at Pratt Institute, New York
1967. Taught at Yale University, School of Art
1968. Taught at Skowhegan School of Painting and Sculpture, Maine
1974–present. Teaches at Brooklyn College, New York

National Endowment for the Arts grant
1969. American Academy of Arts and Letters
1976. Ranger Purchase Prize Award, National Academy of Design
Elected Member of the American Academy of Arts and Letters
1981. First Benjamin Altman Prize (figure), National Academy of Design
1983. Emil and Dines Carlsen Award, National Academy of Design.

The artist lives and works in Brooklyn, New York. He is represented by Davis & Langdale Company, Inc., New York.

AWARDS

1957, 1961. Tiffany Foundation Grant
1958–60. Rome Prize Fellowship
1963. Quinto Maganini Award, Silvermine Grant.
1965. Ingram Merrill Award
1966. Raymond A. Speizer Memorial Prize, Pennsylvania Academy of the Fine Arts

ONE-MAN AND SELECTED GROUP EXHIBITIONS

1962. Tanager Gallery, New York
Group exhibition: Kansas City Art Institute, Missouri (Two-man show with Edwin Dickinson)
1963. Graham Gallery, New York
Group exhibition: "Whitney Annual," Whitney Museum of American Art, New York

1965. Group exhibitions: Albright-Knox Gallery, Buffalo, New York. "Biennial," Corcoran Gallery, Washington, D.C.

1967. Graham Gallery, New York

1969. Graham Gallery, New York

1970. Bard College, Annandale-on-Hudson, New York
Group exhibition: Baltimore Museum

1972. Graham Gallery, New York
Group exhibition: Cleveland Museum of Art

1974. Meredith Long and Company, Houston

1975. Group exhibition: "Trends in Contemporary Realist Painting," Museum of Fine Arts, Boston

1976. Suffolk Community College, Long Island
Group exhibition: "America '76," organized by the U.S. Department of the Interior, and circulated to Corcoran Gallery, Washington, D.C.; Wadsworth Atheneum, Hartford, Connecticut; Institute of Contemporary Art, Boston; The Minneapolis Institute of Arts; Milwaukee Art Center; Fort Worth Art Museum; San Francisco Museum of Modern Art; The High Museum of Art, Atlanta; Brooklyn Museum.

1978. Group exhibitions: "Drawing and Painting on Paper," Kansas City Art Institute, Missouri. "The American Academy in Rome: Five Painters," The American Academy, New York.

1981. Davis & Langdale Company, Inc.

1981–82. Group exhibition: "Contemporary American Realism Since 1960," The Pennsylvania Academy of the Fine Arts, Philadelphia; Virginia Museum of Fine Arts, Richmond; Oakland Museum, California.

1982. William Crapo Gallery, Swain School of Design, New Bedford, Massachusetts

1982–83. Group exhibition: "Contemporary Realist Painting: A Selection," Museum of Fine Arts, Boston

1983. Group exhibitions: "Reallegory," The Chrysler Museum, Norfolk, Virginia. "158th Annual Exhibition," National Academy of Design, New York

PUBLIC COLLECTIONS

Bowdoin College Museum of Art, Brunswick, Maine
Brooklyn Museum
Cleveland Museum of Art, Cleveland, Ohio
Hirshhorn Museum and Sculpture Garden, Washington, D.C.
Hobart and William Smith Colleges, Geneva, New York
Minneapolis Institute of Arts, Minnesota
Museum of Art, The Pennsylvania State University, University Park
Museum of Fine Arts, Boston
Pennsylvania Academy of the Fine Arts, Philadelphia
University of Virginia Museum of Art, Charlottesville
Weatherspoon Gallery, University of North Carolina at Greensboro
Whitney Museum of American Art, New York

Louisa Matthiasdottir

BIOGRAPHY

1917. Born in Reykjavik, Iceland

1930s. Studied painting in Copenhagen, Denmark
Studied with Marcel Gromaire in Paris

1941. Arrived in New York

1943. Began studies with Hans Hofmann at the Eighth Street School

The artist lives and works in New York City. She is represented by Robert Schoelkopf Gallery Ltd., New York.

SELECTED ONE-WOMAN AND GROUP EXHIBITIONS

1948. Jane Street Gallery, New York

1958. Tanager Gallery, New York

1960s. University of Connecticut, Storrs. Windham College, Putney, Vermont.

1964. Robert Schoelkopf Gallery, New York

1966. Robert Schoelkopf Gallery, New York
Group exhibition: Kansas City Art Institute, Missouri (Two-person show with Leland Bell)

1967. Group exhibition: Trinity College, Hartford, Connecticut (Two-person show with Leland Bell)

1968. Robert Schoelkopf Gallery, New York

1969. Robert Schoelkopf Gallery, New York

1970. Albrecht Museum of Art, St. Joseph, Missouri

1972. Robert Schoelkopf Gallery, New York. Litchfield Art Center, Litchfield, Connecticut. Framehouse Gallery, Louisville, Kentucky.

1973. Canton Art Institute, Canton, Ohio

1974. Robert Schoelkopf Gallery, New York

1976. Robert Schoelkopf Gallery, New York

1978. Robert Schoelkopf Gallery, New York. University of New Hampshire, Durham.

1980. Robert Schoelkopf Gallery, New York

1981–82. Group exhibition: "Contemporary American Realism Since 1960," Pennsylvania Academy of the Fine Arts, Philadelphia; Virginia Museum of Fine Arts, Richmond; Oakland Museum, California.

1982. Robert Schoelkopf Gallery, New York
Group exhibition: "Perspectives on Contemporary Realism: Works on Paper from the Collection of Jalane and Richard Davidson," Pennsylvania Academy of the Fine Arts, Philadelphia; Art Institute of Chicago.

PUBLIC COLLECTIONS

Albrecht Gallery of Art, St. Jospeh, Missouri
Hirshhorn Museum and Sculpture Garden, Washington, D.C.

Indiana Art Museum, Bloomington
National Gallery of Art, Reykjavik, Iceland

Trenton Museum, Trenton, New Jersey
Weatherspoon Art Gallery, University of North Carolina at Greensboro

Wayne Thiebaud

BIOGRAPHY

1920. Born in Mesa, Arizona

1936–47. Worked as sign painter, cartoonist, illustrator, and art director

1950–57. Employed as design and art consultant for the California State Fair and Exposition

1951. Received BA from Sacramento State College
Appointed Chairman of the Art Department, Sacramento City College

1952. Received MA from Sacramento State College

1958. Guest instructor, San Francisco Art Institute

1959. Received commission for Sacramento Municipal Utility District Building

1960–present. Professor of Art, University of California at Davis

1967. Summer: Visiting art critic in Painting at Cornell University, Ithaca, New York

1967–68. Commissioned by *Sports Illustrated* to do series of drawings, pastels, and paintings of Wimbledon Tennis Matches, England

1974. Artist-in-residence, Yale University, New Haven, Connecticut

1975. Artist-in-residence, Rice University, Houston
Yosemite Ridge Line commissioned by U.S. Department of the Interior for Bicentennial Exhibition, "America '76."

AWARDS

1964–65. Awarded Creative Art Faculty Fellowship from the University of California at Davis

1967. Selected to represent the United States in the São Paulo (Brazil) Bienal

1972. Selected as National Juror for the National Endowment for the Arts
Selected to represent the United States in "Documenta 5," Kassel, Germany

1973. Awarded distinguished teaching award, "Golden Apple Award," from University of California at Davis
Received Honorary Doctorate from California School of Arts and Crafts, Oakland

1981. Citation from College Art Association of America for most Distinguished Art Studio Teacher, 1980–81

1983. Received Honorary Doctorate of Fine Arts from Dickinson College, Carlisle, Pennsylvania

The artist lives and works in Sacramento, California. He is represented by the Allan Stone Gallery, New York.

ONE-MAN AND SELECTED GROUP EXHIBITIONS

1952. Crocker Art Gallery, Sacramento

1953. Gumps, San Francisco

1954. Artists Cooperative Gallery, Sacramento

1955. San Jose State College, Bakersfield

1957. Sacramento City College

1962. De Young Museum, San Francisco
Group exhibition: "The New Realists," Sidney Janis Gallery, New York

1962–83. Allan Stone Gallery, New York (one-man exhibit each year)

1963. Milan Galleria Schwarz, Milan, Italy

1965. "Figures: Wayne Thiebaud," Stanford University, Stanford, California

1966. Albright Museum, Kansas City, Missouri

1968. "Wayne Thiebaud: Artist in Mid Career," Pasadena Art Museum, California

1969. Group exhibitions: "Aspects of a New Realism," Milwaukee Art Center; Contemporary Art Museum, Houston; Akron Art Institute. "West Coast Art 1945–69," Pasadena Art Museum. "Whitney Annual," Whitney Museum of American Art, New York. "Kompas 4-West Coast USA," Stedlijk van Abbemuseum, Eindhoven, Netherlands.

1970. Crocker Art Gallery, Sacramento

1971. Graphic exhibition, Whitney Museum of American Art, New York.
Group exhibition: "Biennial," Corcoran Gallery, Washington, D.C.

1972. "Wayne Thiebaud—Survey of Painting 1950–1972," California State University Art Galleries, Long Beach
Group exhibitions: "Philadelphia Museum Purchaser's Exhibition," Philadelphia Museum. "70th American Exhibition," Art Institute of Chicago.

1974. Group exhibitions: "Aspects of the Figure," The Cleveland Museum of Art. "Twelve American Painters," Virginia Museum of Fine Arts, Richmond. "Eight from California," National Collection of Fine Arts, Washington, D.C.

1975. Group exhibition: "34th Exhibition Society for Contemporary Art," Art Institute of Chicago

1977. "Retrospective Exhibition," originated by the Phoenix Museum, Arizona, traveled to Oakland Museum, California; University of Southern California; Des Moines Museum; Neuberger Museum, Purchase, New York; Institute of Fine Arts, Boston.

1977. Group exhibition: "Drawings of the 70s," Art Institute of Chicago

1981. One-man exhibit organized by the Walker Art Center, Minneapolis, and circulated to Fort Worth Art Museum, Texas; Museum of Fine Art, St. Petersburg, Florida; Institute of Contemporary Art, University of Pennsylvania, Philadelphia.

1983. Inaugural exhibit, Trout Gallery, Dickinson College, Carlisle, Pennsylvania. "Landscapes and City Views," Crocker Art Gallery, Sacramento.

PUBLIC COLLECTIONS

Albright-Knox Museum, Albany, New York
Albrecht Museum, St. Joseph, Missouri
Library of Congress, Washington, D.C.

Museum of Modern Art, New York
Nelson-Atkins Museum, Kansas City, Missouri
Newark Museum, New Jersey
Oakland Museum, California
Stanford University Art Museum, California
Wadsworth Atheneum, Hartford, Connecticut
Washington Museum of Modern Art, Washington, D.C.
Whitney Museum of American Art, New York
Woodward Foundation

Neil Welliver

BIOGRAPHY

1929. Born in Millville, Pennsylvania
1953. Received BFA from Philadelphia Museum, College of Art
1955–58. Taught at Cooper Union, New York
1955. Received MFA from Yale University, School of Art, New Haven, Connecticut
1955–65. Taught at Yale University, School of Art
1966–present. Teaches at University of Pennsylvania, Philadelphia

AWARDS

1960–61. Morse Fellow
1975. Skowhegan Award for Painting
1983. Guggenheim Fellowship in Painting

The artist lives and works in Lincolnville, Maine. He is represented by Marlborough Gallery, New York, and Brooke Alexander, Inc., New York (prints).

ONE-MAN AND SELECTED GROUP EXHIBITIONS

1952. Alexandra Grotto, Philadelphia
1960. Mirski Gallery, Boston
1962. Stable Gallery, New York
1963. Stable Gallery, New York
Group exhibition: "Annual Exhibition: Contemporary American Painting," Whitney Museum of American Art, New York
1964. Stable Gallery, New York
1967. New Haven Gallery, Connecticut. Tibor de Nagy Gallery, New York.
1968. Tibor de Nagy Gallery, New York
1969. McLeaf Gallery, Philadelphia. Tibor de Nagy Gallery, New York.
1970. Tibor de Nagy Gallery, New York
1971. John Bernad Myers Gallery, New York
1972. John Bernard Myers Gallery, New York
Group exhibitions: "Annual Exhibition: Contemporary American Painting," Whitney Museum of American Art, New York. "The American Landscape," Museum of Fine Arts, Boston.

1973. Parker Street 470 Gallery, Boston
Group exhibition: "Biennial Exhibition: Contemporary American Art," Whitney Museum of American Art, New York.
1974. Fischbach Gallery, New York. University of Rhode Island, Kingston.
1975. Group exhibition: "First International Biennial of Figurative Painting," Tokyo and Osaka, Japan.
1976. Fischbach Gallery, New York. Treat Gallery, Bates College, Lewiston, Maine.
1976–78. Group exhibition: "America '76," organized by the U.S. Department of the Interior, and circulated to Corcoran Gallery, Washington, D.C.; Wadsworth Atheneum, Hartford, Connecticut; Institute of Contemporary Art, Boston; The Minneapolis Institute of Arts; Milwaukee Art Center; Fort Worth Art Museum; San Francisco Museum of Modern Art; The High Museum of Art, Atlanta; Brooklyn Museum.
1977. Munson Gallery, New Haven, Connecticut
Group exhibition: "Eight Contemporary Realists," Pennsylvania Academy of the Fine Arts, Philadelphia; North Carolina Museum of Art, Raleigh.
1978. Brooke Alexander, Inc., New York
1979. Fischbach Gallery, New York
Group exhibition: "The Decade in Review: Selections from the 70s," Whitney Museum of American Art, New York
1980. "Small Studies," Fischbach Gallery, New York
1981. Fischbach Gallery, New York. "Neil Welliver: President's Choice," Visual Arts Gallery, Florida International University, Tamiami, Florida. "Neil Welliver: Paintings and Prints," College of the Mainland Art Gallery, Texas City, Texas.
1981–82. Group exhibition: "Contemporary American Realism Since 1960," Pennsylvania Academy of the Fine Arts, Philadelphia; Virginia Museum of Fine Arts, Richmond; Oakland Museum, California.
1982. "Neil Welliver: Woodcuts and Etchings," Reynolds/Minor Gallery, Richmond, Virginia. "Neil Welliver: Paintings, 1966–80," organized by the Currier Gallery of Art, Manchester, New Hampshire, and circulated to Worcester Art Museum, Massachusetts; Des Moines Art Center, Iowa; Columbus Museum of Art, Ohio; Institute of Contemporary Art, Philadelphia; Virginia Museum of Fine Arts, Richmond.
1983. Marlborough Gallery, New York

PUBLIC COLLECTIONS

American Federation of Arts, New York
Baltimore Museum of Art
Bowdoin College Museum of Art, Brunswick, Maine
Brooklyn Museum
Butler Institute of American Art, Youngstown, Ohio
Carnegie Museum, Pittsburgh, Pennsylvania
Colby College, Waterville, Maine
Currier Gallery of Art, Manchester, New Hampshire
Des Moines Art Center
Grey Art Gallery and Study Center, New York University
Hirshhorn Museum and Sculpture Garden, Washington, D.C.
La Salle College, Philadelphia
Madison Art Center, Madison, Wisconsin
Metropolitan Museum of Art, New York

Museum of Fine Arts, Boston
Museum of Fine Arts, Houston
Museum of Modern Art, New York
New Jersey State Museum, Trenton
North Carolina Museum of Art, Raleigh
Pennsylvania Academy of the Fine Arts, Philadelphia
Philadelphia Museum of Art
Rahr-West Museum, Manitowoc, Wisconsin
Rose Art Museum, Brandeis University, Waltham, Massachusetts
San Francisco Museum of Modern Art
Smith College Museum of Art, Northampton, Massachusetts
Spring Art Association, Springfield, Illinois
Utah Museum of Fine Arts, Salt Lake City
Vassar College Art Gallery, Poughkeepsie, New York
Weatherspoon Art Gallery, University of North Carolina at Greensboro
Whitney Museum of American Art, New York

Credits

W. Auerbach: page 64 (left).
Will Brown: pages 211, 218, 222, 223.
Rudolph Burckhardt: pages 65, 68, 73.
Davis & Langdale Company: pages 154, 158.
eeva-inkeri: pages 14, 15, 18, 19–27, 29–36, 38, 39, 48, 49, 52, 53, 57, 162–179.
Barbara Fendrick Gallery: page 104.
Fischbach Gallery: pages 63, 66, 70, 71, 75, 79, 80, 82, 83, 84, 85, 87.
Allan Frumkin Gallery, New York: 42, 46, 47, 50, 51, 54, 55, 58, 59, 90, 91, 94, 95, 97–102, 105–111.
Timothy Greenfield-Sanders: pages 12, 40, 60, 88, 112, 136, 160, 180, 200.
Bruce C. Jones: page 81.
Marlborough Gallery, New York: 114–125, 127, 130, 134, 135, 206, 207, 210, 214.
Robert E. Mates: pages 128, 129, 132, 202, 203, 205, 209, 212, 213, 216, 220, 221, 224, 225, 226, 227.
Adam Reich: pages 43, 45, 108.
Earl Ripling: page 135.
John D. Schiff: page 4 (right).
Allan Stone Gallery: pages 182, 183, 185, 186, 187, 193 (right), 194, 195, 196, 198, 199.
Joseph Szaszfai: pages 4 (left), 28.
John Tennant: page 215.

PURCHASES AND GIFTS

William Bailey

page 14. *N*, 1964. Collection of Whitney Museum of American Art. Gift of Mrs. Louis Sosland.

page 17. *Head of a Girl (A Portrait)*, 1970. Collection of Yale University Art Gallery. Gift of the artist.

page 18. *Still Life with Rose Wall and Compote*, 1977. Collection of Hirshhorn Museum and Sculpture Garden, Smithsonian Institution. Gift of Mr. and Mrs. Robert Schoelkopf.

page 34. *Mercatale Still Life*, 1981. Collection, The Museum of Modern Art, New York. Purchase.

Jack Beal

page 44. *Still Life with Self-Portrait*, 1974. Valparaiso University Art Collections, Sloan Fund Purchase.

page 46. *Danaë II*, 1972. Collection of Whitney Museum of American Art. Gift of Charles Simon, anonymous donor (and purchase).

page 52. *Prudence, Avarice, Lust, Justice, Anger*, 1977–78. University of Virginia Art

Museum, Charlottesville. Museum purchase.

page 58. *Still Life Painter*, 1978–79. The Toledo Museum of Art, Toledo, Ohio; Gift of Edward Drummond Libbey. © Toledo Museum of Art, 1979.

Philip Pearlstein

page 87. *Female Model in Robe Seated on Platform Rocker*, 1973. San Antonio Museum Association, San Antonio, Texas. Purchase.

page 95. *Female Model on Cast Iron Bed*, 1975. The Art Museum, Princeton University. Anonymous Gift.

page 103. *The Great Sphinx*, 1979. The Toledo Museum of Art, Toledo, Ohio; Gift of American Academy and Institute of Arts and Letters, Hassam and Speicher Purchase Fund. © Toledo Museum of Art, 1979.

page 107. *Two Models in Bamboo Chairs with Mirror*, 1981. The Toledo Museum of Art, Toledo, Ohio; Gift of Edward Drummond Libbey. © Toledo Museum of Art, 1981.

Alex Katz

page 114. *The Red Smile*, 1963. Collection of

Whitney Museum of American Art. Purchase, with funds from the Painting and Sculpture Committee.
page 126. *West Interior*, 1979. The Philadelphia Museum of Art. Gift of the Friends of the Philadelphia Museum of Art.

Lennart Anderson
page 151. *Still Life with Earthenware Vessel*,

1973. Collection of Bowdoin College Museum of Art, Brunswick, Maine. Gift of the American Academy and Institute of Arts and Letters.
page 152. *Nude*, 1961–64. Collection of The Brooklyn Museum, John B. Woodward Memorial Fund.
page 154. *Still Life with Kettle*, 1977. The Cleveland Museum of Art, Purchase,

Wishing Well Fund.

Neil Welliver
page 209. *Cornelius O'Leary, Bishop of Portland, Maine*, 1976. Collection of La Salle College Art Museum, Philadelphia. Given by Victoria Donohoe.

A NOTE ABOUT THE TYPE

The text of this book was set in Palatino, designed in 1948 by the German typographer Hermann Zapf. Named after Giovanbattista Palatino, a writing master of the Italian Renaissance, Palatino was the first of Zapf's typefaces to be introduced to America. Palatino is distinguished by broad letters and vigorous, inclined serifs typical of the work of a sixteenth-century Italian master of writing. The display type is a calligraphic style typeface named Baker Signet after its designer Arthur Baker, a Californian. Baker Signet was one of the fifteen award-winning typeface designs chosen in the 1965 National Typeface Design Competition sponsored by the Visual Graphics Corporation.

The book was composed by Publishers Phototype International Inc. in Carlstadt, New Jersey, and printed and bound by Toppan Printing Co., Ltd. in Japan. The black-and-white illustrations were printed in Duotone, and the color plates in four-color process.

Edited by Carol Southern
Editorial assistance by Kathy Powell
Editorial production by Jean T. Davis
Production supervision by Jane Treuhaft
Design by Hermann Strohbach